IN THE
COMPANY
OF WOMEN

IN THE COMPANY OF WOMEN

Inspiration and Advice from over
100 Makers, Artists, and Entrepreneurs

Grace Bonney

Principal Photography by Sasha Israel

ARTISAN
New York

Library of Congress Cataloging-in-Publication Data

Names: Bonney, Grace, author.
Title: In the company of women / by Grace Bonney ; principal photography by Sasha Israel.
Description: New York, NY : Artisan, [2016] | Includes index.
Identifiers: LCCN 2016013010 | ISBN 9781579655976 (hardback, paper over board)
Subjects: LCSH: Minority businesswomen—United States—Biography. | Businesswomen—United States—Biography. | Minority women executives—United States—Biography. | Women executives—United States—Biography. | Minority women in the professions—United States—Biography. | Women in the professions—United States—Biography.
Classification: LCC HD6057.5.U5 B66 2016 | DDC 338.092/52—dc23 LC record available at https://lccn.loc .gov/2016013010

Design by Doug Turshen

Artisan books are available at special discounts when purchased in bulk for premiums and sales promotions as well as for fund-raising or educational use. Special editions or book excerpts also can be created to specification. For details, contact the Special Sales Director at the address below, or send an e-mail to specialmarkets@workman.com.

Published by Artisan
A division of Workman Publishing Co., Inc.
225 Varick Street
New York, NY 10014-4381
artisanbooks.com

Artisan is a registered trademark of Workman Publishing Co., Inc.

Published simultaneously in Canada by Thomas Allen & Son, Limited

Printed in China

10 9 8 7 6 5 4 3 2

For Julia,
whose company is
the greatest gift
I've ever received

Contents

Introduction

Activist Marian Wright Edelman said, "You can't be what you can't see." Visibility is one of the most powerful tools we have in inspiring people to pursue their dreams and educating them about all the amazing options that exist. My goal with *In the Company of Women* is to provide motivating and relatable examples of all kinds of women running their own businesses, so that any woman, anywhere, can open to a page and see herself reflected.

I started my first business, Design*Sponge (a daily website dedicated to the creative community), in 2004. Running my own business has been the most rewarding—and challenging—part of my life so far. It's taught me to take risks and stand up for what I believe in, and has given me more self-confidence and pride in myself than anything else.

Over the past twelve years of running Design*Sponge, my goals have shifted dramatically, from wanting a place to talk about art and design, to creating a platform for handmade work, to providing advice and resources for the people *behind* that work. Just like people, businesses and their goals change, and now I find myself making professional ideas and inspiration as big a part of what I do as celebrating art and design.

Exactly a decade ago I held my first in-person meet-up for women running their own creative businesses. Frustrated by the knowledge that less than 40 percent of all businesses in the United States are run by women, I wanted to create an event that would work to change those numbers. That series, called Biz Ladies, was an immediate success and has now grown into a regular column on Design*Sponge, spawned countless local groups, and launched companies and collaborations across the country. What I learned from organizing these groups was profound and boils down to this: women *want* to run their own companies and are much more likely to do so if they have the support of other women around them.

I'm proud of what we've done as a community to support these business owners, but in 2014 I had a realization: the majority of women-centered business events, books, and platforms were promoting the *same type* of woman over and over again. These success stories most often belonged to young, straight, white, cisgender women. I am 100 percent in support of any business that's bringing good into the world, but I was acutely aware of how many women (women of color, women from the LGBT community, and differently abled women) weren't being celebrated or included in these discussions.

In the Company of Women highlights over one hundred of the most talented women I know. From young media titans and mother-daughter fashion houses to inspiring painters and poets, the women in this book are shining examples of what we can become if we work hard and support one another. These businesses are diverse: fledgling start-ups to companies with decades of experience, one-woman shows to larger corporations with hundreds of employees.

I traveled across America to interview the vast majority of these women face-to-face. Those moments spent listening and learning have provided me with enough inspiration for decades to come and have motivated me to change the way I run my own business, with a renewed focus on inclusiveness and providing a platform for people to tell their stories in their own voices. The lessons reflected in this book come from lifetimes of experiences in places as far away from my hometown as Nigeria, Australia, and Peru.

While each woman's story is unique, their messages are universal. They've overcome adversity, gone great distances on their own, and learned the power of working together to achieve their goals. In many cases, they have inspired one another, and they are role models for the generation to come. Any one of these women would inspire someone to pursue their passion, but together, they are an undeniable force.

—Grace Bonney

> "Knowing that your success is completely dependent on *you* is beyond scary at times, but I wouldn't change it for the world!"

Danielle Colding

Interior Designer
Brooklyn, NY

What did you want to be when you were a child?

I wanted to be a professional dancer. I danced throughout my childhood, high school, and college. Eventually, I danced professionally for Robert Moses' Kin in San Francisco.

What was the best piece of business advice you were given when you were starting out?

To make sure to hire professionals to do the things you are not good at or knowledgeable about. The key takeaway was that you don't have to be able to do everything on your own. Look to the experts when you need to.

What is your favorite thing about your workspace?

The art. There is an incredible Sol LeWitt mural on one wall [shown at left] and a gallery of some of my favorite fashion and inspiration pictures on the other. It definitely is a "more is more" space, and it feels good to be in it. And now I share it with my husband, so it has become the real center of our home. It's his favorite room in the house too.

What is the biggest sacrifice you've made in starting or running your business?

Security. Owning your own business is a risk. Every day is uncertain and an adventure. If you don't get up and get moving, nothing happens. Knowing that your success is completely dependent on *you* is beyond scary at times, but I wouldn't change it for the world!

What does success mean to you?

My quality of life. And for me, quality of life is having the freedom to make choices that are not fear based. Whether it's the ability to choose the kinds of projects I want to take on and can learn from, or the ability to take a month off to travel. Freedom to choose is the ultimate luxury.

Name the biggest overall lesson you've learned in running a business.

That it is a business before all else. Regardless of the type of business it is, you *must* treat it as a business first and foremost. Even if you are a creative person, the daily nuts and bolts are really about honing your business sense. Without that, it is very difficult to be profitable and thus have creative freedom. It is something I have battled since I started my business.

In moments of self-doubt or adversity, how do you build yourself back up?

I get help. I talk to my friends and colleagues. I am not shy about my vulnerable moments. During those times, I need to talk. I need to hash things out. Wearing my heart on my sleeve certainly doesn't work with everyone, but I have an incredible professional support system that I can rely on in times of adversity.

What quotation inspires and motivates you to be yourself and do what you love?

A quote from Emerson has stuck with me since high school. It has always encouraged me to stay true to my path and to follow my own heart: "It is easy in the world to live after the world's opinion; it is easy in solitude to live after our own; but the great man is he who in the midst of the crowd keeps with perfect sweetness the independence of solitude."

At what point in your life did you first learn about your field of work? What called you to it?

I come from a family of people who have a "good eye," so it was something that was always there. When I was growing up, my house was our oasis from the world, and we spent a ton of time making it beautiful. I am not sure when I first realized it was a job, but I was called to it after ending my career as a dancer. I knew I would always do something creative. And I love working with people, problem solving, and shopping. For me it all just seemed to come together quite naturally.

What does the world need more of? Less of?

The world needs more gratitude and less narcissism.

Which of your traits are you most proud of?

I'm proudest of my resiliency. I have had a tough life and have been through a lot. And I am still standing. And in spite of all the odds, I have found success and happiness.

What is your no-fail go-to when you need inspiration or to get out of a creative rut?

Travel. There is something about getting out of your own space that is transformative. I come alive when I travel. Inspiration pours in. Creativity is sparked. It is magical for me and always leaves me feeling inspired.

What's your favorite thing to come home to after a long day of work?

My dog, Mia. She is always overjoyed to see me. It's unreal. She is a true model for how we all should live. She lives in the moment and enjoys everything that comes her way. It's a real thing of beauty to be around her.

"Success means making meaningful work that promotes inclusivity and community."

Tanya Aguiñiga

Furniture Designer/Maker
Los Angeles, CA

What did you want to be when you were a child?

I longed to be a public servant. I started out wanting to be a teacher, then an astronaut, but then we watched the *Challenger* mission tragedy live in our classroom and that quickly changed my mind. By the end of elementary school I had decided that I wanted to be a firefighter, since they had been the first on the scene when my grandmother passed away.

What was the best piece of business advice you were given when you were starting out?

I've always followed the advice to work *smarter*, not harder. I believe in assessing a situation early in the process to make sure that it will yield success, since time means money. I try not to beat something into the ground, and let go if it's not promising.

What is your favorite thing about your workspace?

My workspace is part of an arts complex in my neighborhood. Because we are a part of one another's community in and out of work, my studio neighbors are generally open to collaboration, friendship, and helping one another's business thrive. I receive a significant amount of business from my studio neighbors each year and I contract them on jobs whenever possible.

What is the biggest sacrifice you've made in starting or running your business?

Stability. Running your own business is full of risks and fluctuation. My practice is multifaceted, with a large focus on community and nonprofit work, and therefore experiences constant highs and lows. The never-ending hustle to get/fund work and then figure out how to execute it well and sustain it is a great source of anxiety for me.

What does success mean to you?

Success to me means being able to continue to do what I love. It means making meaningful work that promotes inclusivity and community.

Name a fear or professional challenge that keeps you up at night.

Money is a constant worry. Not just having the money to keep my business and art practice afloat, but also bringing in enough so I can support my family and keep my wonderful staff gainfully employed. After all that, having enough money for an adequate workspace and to afford the luxury of working on unpaid projects is a constant challenge.

Name the biggest overall lesson you've learned in running a business.

You have to be resourceful, work hard, be kind, and constantly innovate. You never know who a stranger actually is and what they may mean to your business later on, so you have to treat everyone you come across with respect and never burn bridges. You also need to be true to yourself when designing and editing and explore your own story as a source of inspiration, as that is what will give your work more integrity and make you stand out from the crowd.

Name your greatest success (or something you're most proud of) in your business experiences.

Winning the United States Artists Fellowship in Crafts & Traditional Arts has been my greatest accomplishment to date. It is a huge honor to be in such remarkable company, and it pushes me to continue to make work of that caliber.

In moments of self-doubt or adversity, how do you build yourself back up?

I try to share my feelings with everyone in the studio and work through hardships together so we can collectively strategize and move forward. My business is also their business, and anything that can directly affect our livelihood is open to discussion and suggestions.

At what point in your life did you first learn about your field of work? What called you to it?

Having grown up in an environment in Mexico where everything was put to use, I was drawn to artistic expression that was fully functional. My first solo apartment, at the age of eighteen, was above a midcentury furniture store, and I became interested in furniture from staring through the shop windows at night. I walked into the shop one day and asked the owner if I could volunteer at the store. He said you could not volunteer at stores, but that a young lady named Wendy taught furniture design at San Diego State University and I should go study with her. This led to my studying furniture design at SDSU with Wendy Maruyama [page 196] for my bachelor's, and at the Rhode Island School of Design [RISD] with Rosanne Somerson for my MFA. While studying woodworking as an undergraduate, I was introduced to jewelry making/metalsmithing, ceramics, and textiles. All of which led to my further investigations of craft disciplines and their larger connections to our lives through culture, tradition, material use, function, and community.

Knowing what you know now, what would you have done differently when you were first starting out?

I would have taken some business classes, learned more computer programs, looked for grants, and hired an accountant.

What is your personal or professional motto?

I believe that functional works and their imbued context can be used to address roles in the public and domestic spheres. I believe that we can use preconceived notions of objects and materials as design elements to create a platform for discussing greater cultural issues and form meaningful relationships across regions and cultures that have a lasting effect on the direction of society.

Name a woman (or women), past or present, whom you admire or look up to.

I was really lucky to have studied under two amazing women, Wendy Maruyama and Rosanne Somerson, who are leaders in the field of furniture design. Wendy was one of the first two women to receive a master's in furniture design. (Gail Fredell was the other.) Wendy is Japanese American and hearing-impaired and, despite adversity, persisted to become a seminal figure in American furniture design. I also had the great privilege of having Rosanne Somerson as my department head, professor, mentor, and friend. I went to RISD specifically to study under Rosanne, who had become one of my role models in design. When I was a student, Rosanne believed in me more than I believed in myself. Having had two strong women at the helm of my career made me feel like the field was ours for the taking.

> "The pace at which we work allows us to achieve a lot and still have time for fun while designing."

Maya and Teta Gorgoni

Fashion Designers
New York, NY

What did you want to be when you were a child?

Maya: I wanted to be a ballerina or an equestrian.
Teta: As a child, I built a grocery store in my backyard out of cardboard boxes. My siblings and neighborhood friends were my "customers." I was eight years old. So, I've always wanted to be the owner of my own business—that is, a businesswoman.

What was the best piece of business advice you were given when you were starting out?

M: I was advised to grow our business, Royal Jelly Harlem, no faster than I could sustain it physically, emotionally, and financially. Five years later, we are debt-free and have minimized the risks associated with start-ups in an industry that's very competitive.

What does success mean to you?

M: I measure success in terms of the happiness expressed by satisfied customers who wear our clothes.

What is the biggest sacrifice you've made in starting or running your business?

M: I don't feel that I've made any sacrifices; just the opposite is true. I'm doing what I love and enjoy. I think I've been preparing to be this independent businesswoman all my life. I am very lucky to have supportive parents, who are also my role models.

Name a fear or professional challenge that keeps you up at night.

T: I try to make sure I don't bite off more than I can chew, which means scheduling and working at a pace that allows for time to enjoy the day-to-day and that always means a good night's sleep!

Name the biggest overall lesson you've learned in running a business.

M: There is never enough time in a day to accomplish everything, especially when you run a small business like ours. The pace at which we work, however, allows us to achieve a lot and still have time for fun while designing.

In moments of self-doubt or adversity, how do you build yourself back up?

M: Mom.
T: In moments of self-doubt or adversity (and there have been a few), we sort things out as a *team*. We talk issues through, and usually one of us will come up with solutions.

At what point in your life did you first learn about your field of work? What called you to it?

M: I learned how to create and sew clothes from my mother, who made all of my sister's and my clothes. I was designing and making my own clothes at fourteen years old. I've been thinking fashion most of my life and have worked in several areas: as a fashion model, stylist, fashion editor, and designer. The love of fashion is in my blood!

Which of your traits are you most proud of?

M: My determination and that I seldom take no for an answer.

Mother and daughter Teta Gorgoni (right) and Maya Gorgoni

"I have a physical aversion to wasting time."

Tavi Gevinson

Writer, Magazine
Editor in Chief
New York, NY

What did you want to be when you were a child?
An elementary school teacher who did theater at night.

What is your personal or professional motto?
Do what's in front of you.

What is your favorite thing about your workspace?
Switching between the kitchen table by the window and the cozy desk in the corner.

What is the biggest sacrifice you've made in starting or running your business?
What would otherwise have been free time, like after school or postgraduation. But this is what I *wanted* to do with my free time, so it doesn't feel like a sacrifice, just nontraditional.

What does success mean to you?
Having adequately expressed a thought or feeling.

Name a fear or professional challenge that keeps you up at night.
Not filling the day as much as I could have.

Name the biggest overall lesson you've learned in running a business.
Honor audience feedback.

Has learning from a mistake ever led you to success?
There are ongoing conversations with *Rookie* readers, and it's always valuable to hear what they need more and less of, and learn what our blind spots are.

In moments of self-doubt or adversity, how do you build yourself back up?
Self-care, which for me means taking walks alone, journaling, and doing yoga.

What quotation or saying inspires and motivates you to be yourself and do what you love?
"I had always known that life was not appetite and acquisition. In my earnest, angry, good-girl way, I pursued 'meaning.'"—Vivian Gornick

Name your greatest success (or something you're most proud of) in your business experiences.
Rookie Yearbooks One through Four.

Which of your traits are you most proud of?
I have a physical aversion to wasting time. It helps to recognize self-doubt as such.

What was the best piece of business advice you were given when you were starting out?

Own everything.

What's the first thing you do every morning to start your day on the right foot?
Put on a podcast. I need to be engaged with something and listen to people right away.

What's your favorite thing to come home to after a long day of work?
Seinfeld and cereal.

Name a woman (or women), past or present, whom you admire or look up to.
Sally Mann.

"Keep it simple and do the work."

Michele Quan

Ceramicist, Designer
Brooklyn, NY

What did you want to be when you were a child?
At thirteen I spent the summer just outside San Francisco, and my cousin and I said we would drive motorcycles, go to art school, and never get married.

What is your favorite thing about your workspace?
I truly loved my last studio. I called it "Macho Studio." It was in an old brick building in Williamsburg and there was no heat or air-conditioning. The kilns would stall at cone 6 and I would be there from five a.m. till eleven p.m. on firing days. Now I'm in the "Princess Studio" with heat, air-conditioning, a drain in the floor, and a sink. And my firings are usually done by seven p.m.!

What does success mean to you?
To do something one is fulfilled and energized by. Whatever that means to you, in whatever form.

If you were given $100 million, would you run your business any differently? How so?
I'd be working with organizations that provide aid and education.

Name the biggest overall lesson you've learned in running a business.
Keep it simple and do the work.

Has learning from a mistake ever led you to success?

Mistakes always lead somewhere. I've had a couple of big ones, and it took me years to find the jewel hidden in it. But here's an immediate one: Yesterday I was reviewing the "items" in my accounting system so I could enter orders, and decided *once again* to simplify the item codes so I could make overall changes more quickly. I think I finally pared it down to the bare bones, which is going to make it easier on many fronts. Then I thought about how many times and how many *hours* it took for me to get to that point.

Name your greatest success (or something you're most proud of) in your business experiences.

That I strive to be fair and considerate in the process and business of making and selling objects.

What is your personal or professional motto?

Let go or be dragged.

What resources would you recommend to someone starting a creative business?

Take a class or workshop in the basics of running a business. There are logistics to know that will help you avoid having to muddle through trial by fire.

What is your no-fail go-to when you need inspiration or to get out of a creative rut?

Reading.

What tool, object, or ritual could you not live without in your workday?

I need all my tools, but for the last few years it's always, "Where's the good knife?"

Name a woman (or women), past or present, whom you admire or look up to.

So many of them . . . but Patti Smith, Marilynne Robinson, and Pema Chödrön for their beautiful words. My mom and my grandma and my sister.

"I am myself. I refuse to fit into what people want me to be or expect me to be. I stand up for what I believe in and will fight for it."

Preeti Mistry

Chef
Oakland, CA

What was the best piece of business advice you were given when you were starting out?

My wife has really taught me to believe in myself. When I wanted to start my restaurant, Juhu Beach Club, but had no money or deep-pocketed investors, she encouraged me to just do it. Don't wait for someone to hand you a million dollars—just put yourself out there however you can.

What is your favorite thing about your workspace?

Well, a restaurant kitchen more often than not can be a pretty hostile place. Our kitchen believes in *nice*. We help one another, we care about one another, we joke around in a way that is not disrespectful to anyone else. It's a happy place. Also, being my own boss is key to my happiness.

Which of your traits are you most proud of?

I am myself. I refuse to fit into what people want me to be or expect me to be. I stand up for what I believe in and will fight for it.

What is the biggest sacrifice you've made in starting or running your business?

I work all the time. My wife and I talk about the restaurant constantly. It is my life. Sometimes I feel more at home in the restaurant than in my house. So it's time, really. Time with my wife, time with friends and family—all that is sacrificed. I can never truly check out and just be away; you are always still responsible for everything.

What does success mean to you?

This is a question I have been asking myself a lot lately. I used to think it was just financial freedom of some kind, but honestly, that is just what I was raised to believe. If that was all I wanted, I would have become an investment banker. Many people try to convince me that I am successful, but that makes no sense to me. I have so much more to do; there is so much more I want to contribute to the world. I can't put my finger on what "success" truly looks like for me, but I'll let you know when I figure it out.

Name a fear or professional challenge that keeps you up at night.

That I'm a fraud. That somehow I have hoodwinked everyone into believing I'm better than I actually am.

Has learning from a mistake ever led you to success?

This is actually the story of my life. Happy accidents. In the kitchen this is where I get creative and sometimes produce better dishes than ever before. I forgot to order something and have to sub another ingredient, or something burns and we need a new special. It's that pressure that forces my creativity into a place where we then create something even better than the original idea.

In moments of self-doubt or adversity, how do you build yourself back up?

I read shitty Yelp reviews of restaurants that I love and know are amazing. Seriously, I do this sometimes. For me, the cooking becomes meditation: I get in the kitchen and start cooking and tasting, and that reminds me why I'm doing this and that what we are doing is delicious.

In your opinion, what are the top three things someone should consider before starting a business?

1. Do you have a secondary source of income? Financing, a partner with a job, a part-time job, etc.?
2. Is there anything else you are good at or enjoy doing that you could get a job doing and be happy? Because if there is, maybe your creative endeavor could be a hobby?
3. How many birthdays, weddings, holidays, etc., are you willing to miss to realize your dream?

Where were you when you came up with the idea for your business or discovered what you wanted to do?

I was on a road trip from San Francisco to Palm Springs with my wife. I had quit my executive chef job at Google, and we decided to get out of town and take a vacation. I had been thinking of focusing on Indian cuisine and had been experimenting at home for a while. We were wine tasting around Paso Robles and the name hit me—Juhu Beach Club—and then the rest started to fall into place in terms of menu, branding, etc.

Name a woman (or women), past or present, whom you admire or look up to.

Chef Raji Jallepalli. She was an Indian chef who died when she was only fifty-two years old. She was the first to combine Indian and European flavors and techniques back in the 1990s. I had her book when I was just starting out in cooking professionally fifteen years ago, and it was a huge inspiration to me.

> "My best asset cannot be measured or copied or calculated—it's my mojo. I always lay *that* on the table first."

Jodie Patterson

Beauty Entrepreneur
Brooklyn, NY

What did you want to be when you were a child?

When I was in grade school, I wanted to be a teacher. My mom founded and ran a private school in Harlem and I shadowed her all the time—from my perspective, it was the most noble of professions. When I was in high school, I imagined myself being a businesswoman working in a skyscraper in a corner office, wearing a chic Donna Karan suit and high heels. I had this idea I'd have a powerful job. Then after college all I wanted to do was be submersed in literature . . . I thought I'd be a writer.

Name the biggest overall lesson you've learned in running a business.

Winners are losers who got back up. Full stop. If you want something, grab it. Get it. It's yours, damn it.

What was the best piece of business advice you were given when you were starting out?

When I was a little girl, my dad told me, "Your brown skin is so pretty, the world is going to open up for you." What he was saying was not about business, and not really anchored in fact—it was about believing in yourself. It gave me such an amazing surge of confidence. It left me feeling magical, beautiful, and powerful. What my dad taught me and what I've carried with me into business is the appreciation for my aura and myself. My best asset cannot be measured or copied or calculated—it's my mojo. I always lay *that* on the table first.

What is your favorite thing about your workspace?

I work primarily from my home office in Brooklyn because I love the art on my walls. I have mostly portraits, of people I know and some I don't know—they inspire me. I stare at them and think about their lives, their conversations, their dreams. We've had some great company office spaces in the heart of Soho, but nothing compares to my very personal and productive home office.

What is the biggest sacrifice you've made in starting or running your business?

As an entrepreneur, I gave up the "cushion." When I was director of PR for Zac Posen, everything was paid for, everything was covered. But I needed to follow my own dreams—so I left. It's been years since someone else paid for my insurance. Now my family pays for health insurance out of pocket. There were years when I was on Medicaid because I couldn't afford private insurance. It simply made more sense for me to cut costs on myself than to do so on my kids. In fact, I birthed all my children without private insurance. It's tricky and time-consuming to navigate the public-health-care arena and to find good doctors who will take time to really care for you, but that's what we do; we figure it out. That's the sacrifice we make to follow our dreams.

What does success mean to you?

We can be eternally working on the dream, and if we love what we're doing and who we are, we feel accomplished. I rely on six touch points to make myself feel whole: kids, love, business, health, travel, spirituality. If I touch them all *each day*, in varying intensities, I am successful.

If you were given $100 million, would you run your business any differently? How so?

I would hire many more really smart women to deliver in the areas of content, marketing, business development, and research. And I'd invite storytellers to come and share their work with us. Leaders have to nurture health and creativity!

Has learning from a mistake ever led you to success?

I made the mistake of holding on to a business model that wasn't working for far too long. When I started off in beauty, I opened a boutique in downtown New York City. It was gorgeous and marked a turning point in the industry where global beauty and independent brands began to take center stage. It was 2006. Soon after we launched, the economy tanked and spending habits shifted. It proved to be impossible to maintain the store and to grow the business—we were flat and starting to sink. My advisers kept pushing us to close and reopen as a digital store. I thought that would surely be the death of me. I didn't know anything about the digital space. How could I succeed? Plus, I thought I'd lose sight of the customer. Long story short, we closed, and a few years later, I launched DOOBOP, an online beauty destination. It is by far my most successful business to date!

In moments of self-doubt or adversity, how do you build yourself back up?

I'm a mom of five, so I'm used to disappointment, failure, and drama—it's all part of life. But those things that often stop people in their tracks, those "negatives," aren't deterrents for me. I'm no more confident than others, I'm just relentless. When shit is hitting the fan and nothing seems to be working out as planned, I find a project to submerse myself in. I love gritty work, and whenever I'm up to my nose in it, I come out victorious. When business has been slow, I've redesigned my website, learned social media, started a blog, found an agent, and written a book. Creativity leads back to the self and makes one better. I create to stay up.

At what point in your life did you first learn about your field of work? What called you to it?

I learned about the business of beauty from a woman named Madam C. J. Walker, a black Harlemite who made millions by creating a hair relaxer for black women. She was a pioneer in beauty entrepreneurship and launched a multibillion-dollar hair industry. She serviced a community through personal experience and approached her business as an expert in the field. She was smart and intuitive, and had business savvy.

Which of your traits are you most proud of?

I have two characteristics I love most about myself. The first is that I never quit. Never. Exceptionally smart people always surround me, and typically I'm not the smartest in the room. But I have the most grit, the most guts and chutzpah. The second trait I love about myself is that I'm an optimist; I'm always looking ahead with hope.

What's your favorite thing to come home to after a long day of work?

My kids are the only thing that consistently and effortlessly makes me smile. They relax every inch of tension in my body and bring me back to the woman I want to be.

"Success means feeling passionate about what you do."

Linda Rodin

Stylist, Beauty
Entrepreneur
New York, NY

What did you want to be when you were a child?
A mermaid.

What was the best piece of business advice you were given when you were starting out?
To take a business class.

What is your favorite thing about your workspace?
That it is wherever I am. Mostly in my head. Or at home.

What is the biggest sacrifice you've made in starting or running your business?
I didn't make one. I kept all things going all the time.

What does success mean to you?
Success means feeling passionate about what you do.

Name a fear or professional challenge that keeps you up at night.
Things that are out of my control.

Name your greatest success (or something you're most proud of) in your business experiences.
Keeping very long-term relationships.

Name the biggest overall lesson you've learned in running a business.

Patience.

Has learning from a mistake ever led you to success?

I think most things in life are trial and error. So a bit of self-doubt is a good thing.

In moments of self-doubt or adversity, how do you build yourself back up?

I keep moving forward. One step informs the next. For better or for worse.

What quotation or saying inspires and motivates you to be yourself and do what you love?

A lyric from Bob Dylan: "Time is an ocean but it ends at the shore."

At what point in your life did you first learn about your field of work? What called you to it?

I could not find a product that I liked for my skin, so I created my own. I was fifty-nine.

What resources would you recommend to someone starting a creative business?

Your own vision and your own imagination.

What's the first thing you do every morning to start your day on the right foot?

Spend time with my dog and get a delicious cappuccino.

What's your favorite thing to come home to after a long day of work?

Solitude.

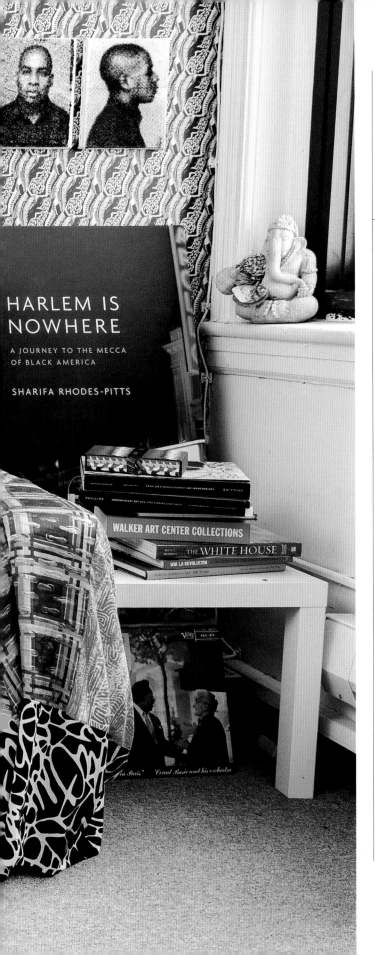

Thelma Golden

Museum Director
and Chief Curator
New York, NY

What did you want to be when you were a child?

I wanted to be a curator! I was obsessed with museums and fascinated by the many ways in which art and artists could teach us.

What characteristic do you most admire in other creative women?

I am always inspired by artists, who are the most creative of people. I have great admiration for their ability to take risks and ask questions.

What does success mean to you?

I define success as being able to match one's passion with a deep sense of purpose.

What is your favorite thing about your workspace?

The way it reflects all the work we do with art and artists, and embodies the Studio Museum's history through the presence of publications, objects, and ephemera from the past and the present.

What is the biggest sacrifice you've made in your career/line of work?

I've never been able to successfully have a hobby.

Has learning from a mistake ever led you to success?

I think in every decision one makes, there is a learning opportunity. Sometimes decisions have outcomes that can be difficult—I guess you can call that a mistake, but I prefer to think of it as a learning opportunity!

Name a fear or professional challenge that keeps you up at night.

I like to think of challenges as opportunities— opportunities to think differently and create something new. And I welcome the charge I get from acknowledging them as such.

What quotation or saying inspires and motivates you to be yourself and do what you love?

"I am deliberate / and afraid / of nothing." —Audre Lorde

What is your no-fail go-to when you need inspiration or to get out of a creative rut?

My husband, Duro Olowu, who is a brilliant designer.

What would you tell yourself ten to twenty years ago that you wish you knew then?

That what seem like urgent and immediate obstacles will recede greatly with time.

What is your personal or professional motto?

"Start where you are. Use what you have. Do what you can." —Arthur Ashe

Where were you when you came up with the idea for your business or discovered what you wanted to do?

I decided to be a curator after many visits to museums, and when I was about ten years old, a family friend gave my brother and me the board game Masterpiece, which included reproductions of works of art from the collection of the Art Institute of Chicago. I had no interest in the game, but I was very happy arranging and rearranging the playing cards and making "exhibitions" with them.

What does the world need more of?

I always think the world could use more art.

What tool, object, or ritual could you not live without in your workday?

I love walking to work down 125th Street and being fully immersed in the neighborhood of Harlem. I'm so inspired by, and so lucky to live and work in, this historic, vibrant, diverse community.

Name a woman (or women), past or present, whom you admire or look up to.

First Lady Michelle Obama.

**In moments of self-doubt or adversity,
how do you build yourself back up?**

*I think about all the
mentors, friends, and
colleagues who have
worked, achieved, survived,
and thrived, and I take
great inspiration from
their stories.*

> **"Success for me is the legacy you leave behind when you're gone from this earth."**

Cy Lauz

Lingerie Designer
Long Island, NY

What did you want to be when you were a child?

I wanted to be everything from an artist to a veterinarian to a lawyer. In college I set my sights on being a veterinarian. I was three years into working at a veterinary clinic in Hoboken, New Jersey, when I was bitten in the face by a dog and attacked by a cat the next day. That ended my aspirations very quickly!

What was the best piece of business advice you were given when you were starting out? (Or a piece of advice you're glad you ignored?)

The piece of advice I'm glad I ignored would be, "There is no market for the transgender community. You're wasting your time!"

What is your favorite thing about your workspace?

That it's located in my home. Luckily, I live in a home that I feel safe in and that inspires me, and it's a quick commute to the "office."

What is the biggest sacrifice you've made in starting or running your business?

As my company is a start-up, my biggest sacrifice would be investing my own money. At times I couldn't make rent, because I opted to use the money I had to further Chrysalis Lingerie.

What does success mean to you?

I think defining success is a very personal thing. For me it's the legacy you leave behind when you're physically gone from this earth. Did you help anyone? Did you contribute to the betterment of your community or society as a whole?

Name a fear or professional challenge that keeps you up at night.

The biggest professional challenge for me would be trusting anyone other than myself.

In moments of self-doubt or adversity, how do you build yourself back up?

Self-doubt is my kryptonite, but adversity gives me life! I consider myself an underdog. I romanticize the idea of the whole world being against you and you have nothing but yourself and sheer will to depend on. I mean, that's the stuff superheroes are made of! I usually try to relive moments when this underdog archetype fueled me, especially moments from my childhood. I think, If I got through that as a child, this is nothing!

Name your greatest success (or something you're most proud of) in your business experiences.

Acknowledging and honoring that I am my most valuable resource.

What is your no-fail go-to when you need inspiration or to get out of a creative rut?

I put on my most comfortable shoes, take the train downtown to the East Village, and walk! I start from there and work my way up to 116th Street in Spanish Harlem. New York City is all the inspiration anyone could ever need.

Name a woman (or women), past or present, whom you admire or look up to.

It may sound corny, but I really do admire all women. I realized how powerful women are when I was a freshman in college in sociology 101. The lecture that day was to the effect of "when you change the lives of women, you also change family life—and when that core of family values is changed, you've changed the world forever." As a trans woman I now experience what it's like to be a woman today, and to be able to shine while living in a world that seeks to dim your light is a feat in and of itself.

> "Most times my inner voice tells me in a flash what I want and need, and whom to trust. I'm learning to honor that inner voice."

Lisa Hunt

Designer, Artist
Brooklyn, NY

What did you want to be when you were a child?

I went through several phases as a child: ballerina, *Solid Gold* dancer, construction worker, bus driver. I remember telling my grandmother I wanted to be an artist and her telling me I would starve. Scarred for life! I also remember sitting at my bedroom window and watching the construction of a new house next door. I was fascinated as I watched the construction workers laying bricks that eventually made a wall. I thought, What an amazing job to be outside all day in the sun getting dirty and making a house! Making something useful with your own two hands. I told my mom I wanted to be a construction worker! Now as I sit in my sunny studio designing and making, with my own two hands, useful and beautiful things for the home, I can't help but be reminded of my childhood admiration of construction workers.

What was the best piece of business advice you were given when you were starting out?

I'd say the best piece of advice was to be clear on aligning what your business is and how much time you're willing to dedicate to it.

What is the biggest sacrifice you've made in starting or running your business?

The biggest sacrifice would be time. Leisure time, time with family and friends, time for yourself.

What does success mean to you?

Success to me is the ability to work toward your dreams while being appreciative of and present where you are. You have to enjoy the journey— life is too short not to.

Name a fear or professional challenge that keeps you up at night.

I was really shy as a child and at times I can still be an introvert. My father was in the air force and we moved around a lot, so I was always the "new girl." My way of coping was to blend in and be observant. As a business owner I know the importance of being able to network and make personal connections with your customers. It's something I work on every day.

Name the biggest overall lesson you've learned in running a business.

Trust your instincts! There's nothing worse than realizing that your first instincts were right and that second-guessing led to a costly mistake. As women we're taught to second-guess ourselves and to look to others for direction and guidance. Most times my inner voice tells me in a flash what I want and need, and whom to trust. I'm learning to honor that inner voice.

What quotation or saying inspires and motivates you to be yourself and do what you love?

My mother always told me to be true to myself, and that's stuck with me and helps me in my vision for my company. Now, of course it's important to know who your true self is and to like her, a lot! Honor her, make friends with her, support her, give her a break when she needs one, and love her unconditionally!

What is your personal or professional motto?

Not to take myself too seriously, and to remember to laugh and have fun.

What's your favorite thing to come home to after a long day of work?

My couch! I love my couch—I bought her about fifteen years ago, and she's hanging in there. She's big and cushy and perfect for napping. She's seen me through a lot of ups and downs over the years.

If you were magically given three more hours per day, what would you do with them?

I would be more physically active. I spend a lot of hours in front of a desk, and riding my bike or even taking a walk is a luxury that I would like to allow myself.

In moments of self-doubt or adversity, how do you build yourself back up?

I am nothing if not resilient! I've nurtured the ability to feel nervous but jump in anyway and know that if I make a mistake or misjudgment, I have the smarts to work things out. It wasn't always like that—with age comes wisdom.

> "My motto is *La cultura cura*, or 'culture heals.'"

Amalia Mesa-Bains

Artist, Curator, Author
San Juan Bautista, CA

What did you want to be when you were a child?
I always wanted to be an artist.

What was the best piece of business advice you were given when you were starting out? (Or a piece of advice you're glad you ignored?)
I was once told to concentrate on only my own artwork and not to write about other artists. It was bad advice, as I learned so much trying to understand the work of other women artists.

What is the biggest sacrifice you've made in starting or running your business?
To do my artwork I often have had to work within the context of my teaching and family, so I sacrifice time.

What does success mean to you?
When I was younger, I thought success was about big, prestigious exhibitions. But as the years have passed, I feel even more successful when my work, both art and writing, is valuable to a younger generation, a legacy of sorts.

Name the biggest overall lesson you've learned in running a business.
In all my professional work I have learned the value of keeping your commitments and of building a network of friends and colleagues.

Has learning from a mistake ever led you to success?
I was working on a large triptych mirror with an image partially emerging from the mirror where I had scraped off the backing. The artwork was for an installation of the *studiola* of a seventeenth-century Mexican nun, Sor Juana Inés de la Cruz, who was punished for her intellectual pursuits. The mirror slipped off the worktable and crashed to the floor, with all the cracks emerging from her forehead, so I meticulously glued the mirror slivers back into place, cutting my fingers and leaving bloody smudges. I sent the piece off hoping they would accept it, and it was so well received because the museum curator thought I had done it on purpose to symbolize her suffering. They ended up buying the whole installation for the museum, and it has remained one of my most successful pieces.

Name your greatest success (or something you're most proud of) in your business experiences.
My artwork *An Ofrenda for Dolores del Rio* was acquired by the American Art Museum at the Smithsonian in 1995 and I received a MacArthur Fellowship in 1992.

What does the world need more of?
The world needs more compassion and justice.

What is your personal or professional motto?
La cultura cura, or "culture heals."

What tool, object, or ritual could you not live without in your workday?
Coffee time in the morning and meditation and prayer in the evening.

Name a woman (or women), past or present, whom you admire or look up to.
There are several, including my mentor, Yolanda Garfias Woo; Judy Baca, the muralist; and Marta Moreno-Vega, director of the Caribbean Cultural Center.

> "Every day I feel successful because I wake up doing what I love."

Malene Barnett

Textile Designer
Brooklyn, NY

What did you want to be when you were a child?

When I was in the third grade, my mother enrolled me in a program for artistically gifted children; I played the violin and piano and danced. Back then, I really wanted to be a dancer, perhaps because my younger sister and I loved music videos and practiced reenacting the choreography. Eventually, I dropped the violin and piano, and after I discovered my true passion—art—I only danced for fun.

What was the best piece of business advice you were given when you were starting out?

I have been bootstrapping my business, Malene B, from the start, and after operating for a few years I had the opportunity to introduce my growth strategy to angel investors. One of those investors advised me to continue bootstrapping and not partner with an investor, sharing that once the "big deal" came through, the money would be all mine. To this day, her advice is still sage and my business continues to grow organically with me reaping its benefits.

What is your favorite thing about your workspace?

My home office is in a Queen Anne–style town house in Brooklyn, New York, and was a third bedroom that I had converted to an open loft space. My walls are painted in shades of tangerine, so even in the middle of winter it looks and feels like summer.

What does success mean to you?

Success is living my life based on purpose. Every day I feel successful because I wake up doing what I love. My greatest hope is that my work and life inspire others to live out their passions too.

Name the biggest overall lesson you've learned in running a business.

I have learned that making beautiful products is great, but if they don't sell, you don't have a business—it's a hobby. The design business is not about creating the best design; rather, it's about creating design solutions for people who seek to live a certain way. Understanding this taught me to remove my personal taste from creating and instead look at my talent as a tool to share with our global community.

What quotation or saying inspires and motivates you to be yourself and do what you love?

"Success occurs when preparation meets opportunity." With this as a mantra, I continue to prepare my business so it can be ready for boundless opportunities.

What tool, object, or ritual could you not live without in your workday?

My iPhone. I use my phone to access files, post to social media, take pictures, listen to music . . . the list is endless. I don't know how I did what I do before having a great mobile device.

If you were magically given three more hours per day, what would you do with them?

I would play my favorite reggae and soca songs, then freestyle design whatever comes to mind.

> "Be authentic. Own your work style and don't ever think you have to change who you are to be successful."

Cheryl Day

Baker, Author
Savannah, GA

What did you want to be when you were a child?

I wanted to be an actor, photographer, and writer. I've wanted to live a creative life for as long as I can remember.

What was the best piece of business advice you were given when you were starting out?

My sister was an incurable entrepreneur, and she taught me many of my most valued lessons in business and in life. She told me to always be consistent. In the early days when business was slow in the late afternoons and I had already worked a long day, it was tempting to hang the "gone fishing" sign, but I always remembered her words.

I think it is fantastic advice for both the start-up and the established business owner to not rest on your laurels. Whether it is the hours you are open for business or the frequency in posting on a blog, let people know they can depend on you. I believe that being consistent has been one of the best ways to build our reputation and to grow our business.

What is your favorite thing about your workspace?
The bakery space itself! It truly is a reflection of who I am. From the huge factory windows that we salvaged from an old building in Savannah to our work kitchen, it's a blessing and a luxury to work in a space that we created down to the smallest detail.

What does success mean to you?
Success for me is realizing that I have achieved more in my lifetime than any of the women in my family who have set the groundwork before me. I have been afforded opportunities that were not available to them, and I know they would be very proud to see how far I've come. To think it all started with my great-grandmother Muddy, who had an incredible work ethic and was an excellent cook and entrepreneur in Dothan, Alabama.

Name a fear or professional challenge that keeps you up at night.
Instead of counting sheep, I fall asleep walking through my schedule for the next day to make sure everything will run as smoothly as possible. Will everyone show up for work? How can I make something better than I made it yesterday? Did I remember to order everything I need for the day? These are all things that keep me up at night.

Name the biggest overall lesson you've learned in running a business.
Be authentic. Own your work style and don't ever think you have to change who you are to be successful. As one of my dear friends put it, "Choose your lane and keep your eye on success."

In moments of self-doubt or adversity, how do you build yourself back up?
For me, running a business is stepping out in faith every day. I surround myself with folks with positive energy who are moving forward. No "Negative Nellies" are allowed in my world.

Which of your traits are you most proud of?
I have been told that I am a trailblazer and I have a knack for spotting trends.

Name your greatest success (or something you're most proud of) in your business experiences.
I am thankful that I attracted a loving partner in business and in life. I am proud that together we coauthored two bestselling cookbooks, created a food landmark, and were named semifinalists for a James Beard award in the category for Outstanding Bakers, all on a shoestring budget.

What resources would you recommend to someone starting a creative business?
I would suggest immersing yourself in the culture of your trade in any way you can. Seek out a mentorship or an apprenticeship or join professional organizations (and don't forget to learn the business side of things too!). I think it is important to take an honest look at yourself and what it takes to be successful in your field of interest.

What is your personal or professional motto?
This or something better. When things don't go your way, it's hard to understand. I have grown to know that there is always something better just around the corner.

What's your favorite thing to come home to after a long day of work?
Spending time with my husband and our dog, Ella Day, is my favorite way to unwind. Family is everything for me, and they are mine.

Name a woman (or women), past or present, whom you admire or look up to.
Edna Lewis, the "Grande Dame" of Southern cooking, who ensured that Southern food would not be lost to history. She inspired me to become a Southern baker, and I hope to do the same for others.

If you were magically given three more hours per day, what would you do with them?
I would get back that free time that I lost when dreaming about, opening, and running a business.

> "We are trained to fit in, assimilate, and blend in. I'm always enamored of women who overcome that."

Janet Mock

Author, Television Host
New York, NY

What did you want to be when you were a child?

When I was younger, I thought I wanted to be a lawyer, an everyday crusader who slayed people with my didactic speeches and pencil skirts. This was largely because of my fascination with Gregory Peck in *To Kill a Mockingbird* and with *Ally McBeal*.

What characteristic do you most admire in other creative women?

The audacity to do something different and embody their own difference. We are trained to fit in, assimilate, and blend in, so I'm always enamored of women who overcome that training and just stick out.

What does success mean to you?

I define success in writing and hosting by asking two questions: Are you able to show up, be yourself, and tell the truth no matter what? And are you able to create a space where other people feel welcomed to share their truth?

What is your favorite thing about your workspace?

My favorite thing is being faced with a blank page and having endless possibilities to say what is on my mind, uncover truths, and share myself with the world, whether that blank page is an essay, a show script, or a book project.

What is the biggest sacrifice you've made in your career/line of work?

I've sacrificed a lot when it comes to time, particularly the time that is required to sit in community with friends, with loved ones. As my career has grown and demands have pulled at me, I have had to become more vigilant about scheduling time for me and my people.

Has learning from a mistake ever led you to success?

A mistake I made at the beginning of my public writing career was being a bit too open and transparent. I learned that I needed to create boundaries—clear and exacting—that I would not cross until I truly was ready to share things publicly. It was an early mistake that required me to realize that not all of me was up for public consumption.

Name a fear or professional challenge that keeps you up at night.

A consistent fear is: Am I doing enough? Does my work really matter? These thoughts plague many people, and I see it as common. What I always have to remind myself is that it is okay to recognize that doubt but that it cannot stay for long. It's a visitor that ensures I am always cognizant of where I am with myself and my work.

In moments of self-doubt or adversity, how do you build yourself back up?

I surround myself with a small group of people who don't expect anything from me but to be fully myself. They love me not despite of but because I am myself.

What does the world need more of? Less of?

The world needs more listening and less talking.

> "I'm never worried about having enough inspiration. I'm worried that one lifetime will never be enough to execute it all."

Genevieve Gorder

Interior Designer,
Television Host
New York, NY

What did you want to be when you were a child?

I wanted to be a dancer and a dermatologist because when I was four, I thought that I was *really* good at dancing and loved to pick . . . anything. By five, I had blended these two titles officially. And when people asked me what I wanted to be, I said very simply, "A dancing doctor."

What was the best piece of business advice you were given when you were starting out?

There were so many. In design school a professor told me to always "show them your fifth idea. The first few concepts were all shared by every designer . . . get to your weird place, your special place, the fifth, sixth, seventh concept. That's when gold appears." I liked that advice a lot. In television, a producer once told me, "Don't talk over all the silent moments. Let them hang like fruit, even when it gets uncomfortable. The person you're asking questions of will inevitably fill the void with a more honest self."

What is your favorite thing about your workspace?

It's not the architecture or even the geography of it. I just love that it's mine. I share so much of myself, my design, my time with the world. This is the one space where I can be quiet, where I can create like I did as a child or an art student. It's not judged, it's just mine.

What is the biggest sacrifice you've made in starting or running your business?

Time . . . and my twenties. I think when it's a passion, it's hard to call anything you do for it a sacrifice, but I know I've missed many important events and happenings in my family and my own life because of the lifestyle that comes with my career. Television eats life, but it also gives a richness of experiences that just can't be duplicated by any other profession, other than film.

What does success mean to you?

I like this question because it's hard. The simplest answer I can think of is to be able to live my imagination and give it away to as many people as possible in one lifetime. I'm never worried about having enough inspiration. I'm worried that one lifetime will never be enough to execute it all.

Name a fear or professional challenge that keeps you up at night.

The juggle. How do I keep all the balls in the air and make sure they are perfectly polished?

Name the biggest overall lesson you've learned in running a business.

You have to stretch to grow. And surround yourself with not only talented people whom you can delegate to, but also with good souls. Without grace and kindness, your skills are unimportant to me.

Has learning from a mistake ever led you to success?

It's all trial and error, isn't it? As a Midwesterner, as a woman, as a freelancer, as a designer with an atypical job, as a very caring person, I tend to say yes to everything. I want to please, I want to work hard, I want everyone to just be happy. If you do that too long, you break because you forget to take care of you. I've learned to say

no primarily as a mother and now as an experienced member of the design community. No is powerful. When you can say no, you have worth. I've learned that by saying no to certain jobs and other aspects of life, I can be more balanced, and often offers that are more valuable quickly follow.

At what point in your life did you first learn about your field of work? What called you to it?

My childhood would have been a renovation show if there had been a camera present. We restored and renovated Victorian homes in Minneapolis throughout the '80s and early '90s. I didn't grow up with interior designers or even an idea of who did that job. It wasn't until college when I was studying international affairs with the hopes of going into the foreign service one day that I happened to take my first graphic design course as an art requirement. I was always good at and very much into the arts but didn't know that it could or would become my job. With that course alone, it was as if the sky had parted and I saw the light . . . I knew at eighteen years old that I would be doing this for the rest of my life. As a designer, it's as though you're the conductor of a highly aesthetic orchestra; it was everything. And still is.

What resources would you recommend to someone starting a creative business?

1. Embrace social media completely. It is the most incredible tool to feed your audience, to engage, and to advertise (skillfully). You should give a portion of every day to do this as a creative business owner. Follow people in the field; follow people who are really, really good at it to learn your craft.

2. Create a "no assholes" policy. Nobody you work with or hire can have this quality. Life is too short and we are too sensitive to suffer unkind people. Live kind; your work will show it.

3. Travel to fill your tanks. We need to see harder than everyone else. If we're not seeing new life, we repeat ourselves. It is not a luxury—it is a necessity.

> "We must always improvise in life. Flexibility allows for creativity."

Carla Fernández and Cristina Rangel

Fashion Designers
Mexico City, Mexico

What was the best piece of business advice you were given when you were starting out?

Cristina: Be patient and be humble. Surround yourself with people who can advise you.

Carla: When I was fourteen years old, my parents encouraged me to start working summers so I could pay for whatever I wanted. I started working with friends and learned very young the importance of having a job.

What is your favorite thing about your workspace?

CR: There is a particular chaos in our workshop that reminds me we must always improvise in life and that flexibility allows for creativity.

What is the biggest sacrifice you've made in starting or running your business?

CR: Economic stability. I was lucky enough to have financial support from family during the first few years to be able to take the leap into entrepreneurship.

CF: I work day and night, and even my vacations are tied in to work. However, I am very lucky to have a job that I really love, which turns sacrifice into pleasure.

What does success mean to you?

CR: I always thought Carla and I would be successful (and I think to some extent we already are). We recognize that the legacy of our Mexican culture is our most valuable asset. Through hard work and with the support of others in our culture, we will be able to create the Mexico that we all dream of—one of fairness, honesty, quality, and diversity.

In moments of self-doubt or adversity, how do you build yourself back up?

CR: I usually end up convincing myself what is real and what I tend to forget: if we fail, if this company doesn't succeed, I will be okay; failure is part of life. I will have learned so much from the years invested in this company that any other endeavor will be another stepping-stone toward success.

CF: I just think about all the people who work on our projects and how we depend on the strength of all of us. We are here to collaborate and help one another.

Knowing what you know now, what would you have done differently when you were first starting out?

CF: I would have searched for my partner, Cristina, ten years before.

> "It's helpful to see successful, creative women flourishing because of boundaries they have set, rather than in spite of them."

Samin Nosrat

Chef, Author
Berkeley, CA

What did you want to be when you were a child?

As a little girl, I adored and admired my aunt Ziba, who lived with us while she was in college. She had a part-time job shelving books in the university library. So I wanted to be a librarian, just like her, when I grew up.

In high school, my English teacher and cross-country coach changed my life. Tom Dorman was the first feminist I ever met. He taught me to change a tire, to love the natural world, and to question authority. He also gave me a subscription to *The New Yorker* and told me that I could write. Ever since then, I've wanted to be a writer. Even as I began my cooking career, I never abandoned the idea that one day I'd write books.

What characteristic do you most admire in other creative women?

Boundaries, because I have very few and am constantly struggling with them. It's helpful to see successful, creative women flourishing because of boundaries they have set, rather than in spite of them.

What is your favorite thing about your workspace?

Seeing my kitchen full of beautiful, meaningful, and useful things inspires me daily. There are the items I've collected from all around the world: wooden spoons from Cuba and Mexico; brass and bronze pasta-making tools from Italy; handmade spice boxes from Pakistan. And then there are all the gifts from friends—beautiful ceramics from Japan, Peru, and Colombia; a hand-hewn cutting board made from the wood of a tree I loved to sit beneath; a cleaver Alice Waters gave me from the oldest knife shop in China after we traveled together to Beijing for an event. Every time I pass through my little kitchen, I'm reminded of all the serendipitous ways in which my work, life, and loved ones influence and improve one another.

If you were given $100 million, would you run your business any differently? How so?

Yes! I'd make three basic changes:

1. I'd build a beautiful, inspiring workspace that could function as both my writing office and teaching and test kitchen, as well as a place where I could host larger gatherings, such as book signings and special dinners. There'd be lots of natural light, high ceilings, art installations by some of my favorite artists, an outdoor wood-burning oven and grill, vegetable and flower gardens, and, most definitely, a napping spot.
2. I'd hire a support staff, and support them. I easily get lost in the nitty-gritty of running a small business. I'd bring on hardworking people who could take care of the stuff at which I'm not adept, so I could focus on the work that only I can do. From designers to accountants to teachers to someone to manage everyone, I'd look to hire intelligent, talented, independent people who'd be stoked about working together toward a central goal—teaching, inspiring, and encouraging everyone to cook and prioritize the act of coming together for a meal. And I would take really good care of them as their employer.
3. I'd found a nonprofit organization. I've always admired the work of 826 Valencia, the nonprofit established by Dave Eggers to support under-resourced students with their writing skills. I loved how he used his newfound literary notoriety to recruit all his well-known writer friends to participate and support 826, in turn bringing all sorts of attention to the organization. I believe it's just as vital to support kitchen literacy in our youth, and would be thrilled to use some of my magic money to establish a culinary analogue to 826 and get everyone I know involved.

In moments of self-doubt or adversity, how do you build yourself back up?

Therapy.

Which of your traits are you most proud of?

Boundless curiosity.

What does the world need more of? Less of?

In the words of the tragically late, luminous artist Susan O'Malley, "Less Internet, More Love."

What quotation or saying inspires and motivates you to be yourself and do what you love?

"Imagination is better than a sharp instrument. To pay attention, this is our endless and proper work." —Mary Oliver

What is your no-fail go-to when you need inspiration or to get out of a creative rut?

Jumping in the ocean.

What's the first thing you do every morning to start your day on the right foot?

Take my antidepressants.

Name a woman (or women), past or present, whom you admire or look up to.

Alice Waters. Julia Child. Elena Ferrante. Joan Didion. And my congresswoman Barbara Lee, who was the sole member of the U.S. Congress to vote against the authorization of use of force following the September 11, 2001, attacks.

If you were magically given three more hours per day, what would you do with them?

Sleep.

> "From a young age we were both taught and shown that it's okay to be different, and that has helped us to get where we are today."

Elise Kornack and Anna Hieronimus

Chef, Restaurateurs
Brooklyn, NY

What did you want to be when you were a child?
Elise: A doctor.
Anna: A vet.

What was the best piece of business advice you were given when you were starting out?
E: Trust your vision and be patient.
A: My mom always says to me, "If you're doing your best, that's all you can do."

What is your favorite thing about your workspace?
E: The natural light; most commercial kitchens don't have any natural light at all.

Anna Hieronimus (left) and Elise Kornack

What is the biggest sacrifice you've made in starting or running your business?

E: Free time. When you own your own place/start your own business and are your own boss, much of your time spent away from work is spent . . . doing work.

Name a fear or professional challenge that keeps you up at night.

E: Our business flooded a few years ago when we were on our honeymoon. We came back to a destroyed restaurant and two months' worth of renovations to get back up and running. Any time we leave town we are always concerned something similar will happen again. Thank God it hasn't!

Name the biggest overall lesson you've learned in running a business.

E: Most of the time things won't turn out the way you expect, and that's usually not a bad thing. Don't let go of your goals, but let go of your expectations.

A: Be patient, in all ways.

Has learning from a mistake ever led you to success?

A: At the very beginning, when we first opened our restaurant, we wanted the tasting menu to be served at a communal table—so that's the setup we chose. After the first few months of dinner service, we realized that this particular setup wasn't the most comfortable one for our customers. Sometimes you need to stray from your original point of view or plan and do something different—needless to say, it was for the best and made both our customers and us a lot happier. After our first few months in business, we realized you have to constantly put yourself in your customers' shoes in order to provide the best experience you can.

What is your personal or professional motto?

A: When we have a rough night of work or a chaotic dinner service, our motto is, you have to push through. Everything comes to an end eventually and sometimes you just have to push through an experience that makes you uncomfortable in some way.

Name your greatest success (or something you're most proud of) in your business experiences.

E: Earning a Michelin star in 2015. It's something that every chef dreams of—it feels like the greatest honor and blessing.

A: Making it work. People challenged us in the beginning, laughed at us, thought what we were doing was "weird" because it was different, but we made it work; we now own a successful business that is fully functional and running—and running *well*. So in that sense, I feel we really came out on top.

In moments of self-doubt or adversity, how do you build yourself back up?

E: We look to our families for advice and guidance, as they are our unconditional support system.

Where were you when you came up with the idea for your business or discovered what you wanted to do?

A: My parents live on fifty acres of land in Maryland. That's where we were when we originally came up with the concept of Take Root. Elise had just left Aquavit, I was in between jobs, and we had decided to take a few weeks away from New York City to decompress and begin thinking about what was next for both of us, workwise. We still have a leaf that we found on that very "woods walk" the day the idea for Take Root came into being.

What tool, object, or ritual could you not live without in your workday?

E: The ritual of beginning and ending our day together. In the morning over a cup of coffee, gearing up for the day—at night, with a glass of wine, recapping the happenings.

Name a woman (or women), past or present, whom you admire or look up to.

A: The women in our families—my sister and our mothers. They are all creative, hardworking, and strong willed—marching to the beats of their own drums. From a young age we were both taught and shown that it's okay to be different, and that has helped us to get where we are today.

“The world needs more
questions and fewer
answers.”

Kate Bornstein

Author, Performer,
Activist
New York, NY

What did you want to be when you were a child?

To be a girl, to be on television, and to be a
superhero in a comic book. Happy me! Girl . . .
done, 1986. My first TV appearance was on
Geraldo Rivera's talk show, 1992-ish, and my
most recent appearance was on *I Am Cait* with
Caitlyn Jenner. And also in the early '90s, author
Rachel Pollack based the *Doom Patrol* character of Coagula, aka Kate Godwin, on me—she's
a transsexual lesbian with superpowers that liq-
uefy solids and vice versa. It's taken me a lifetime
to develop them, but yes, those are my powers.

**What characteristic do you most admire in other
creative women?**

Creative women understand that "the show must
go on," so they never stop—well, not for long.
No matter the creative field, there are always
daunting barriers to making art. Procrastination,
self-doubt, and discouraging words from others
top my list of what slows me down.

What does success mean to you?

Success is when my readers and audience get the
jokes, cry at the sad parts, and gasp in wonder;
they have to do all three—laugh, cry, and gasp—
before I believe I've succeeded. As a human being,

the times I've felt successful have been the times when I've been able to say, "I've done enough."

If you were given $100 million, would you run your business any differently? How so?
I've been dreaming about this one for years, so answering this succinctly isn't a problem. I'd completely switch gears in my life. I'd buy myself an old hotel down the Jersey Shore; turn it into a live-in school for the creative arts; hire lots of my cool, freaky, art-making friends; and open it up to at-risk youth.

What is the biggest sacrifice you've made in your career/line of work?
Mainstream recognition. I'm a brat, a freak, a pervert, and a mad thing. There've been half a dozen or so times in my career when I could have chosen a more conservative path that would have given me a mainstream breakthrough. But it always came with the same conditions: clean up, don't talk about the scary stuff, and don't make it too sexy. Well, I write mostly for teens, freaks, and other outlaws—I consider them my family. Scary and sexy are my family's lifeblood, and we mostly only clean up for one another.

Name a fear or professional challenge that keeps you up at night.
I asked my girlfriend if she could name what it is that keeps me up at night, and she rattled off a long list of things ranging from social activism to beauty secrets. She started to name some more stuff when I asked her to please stop. So thanks. Trying to answer this question is going to keep me up at night.

In moments of self-doubt or adversity, how do you build yourself back up?
I live with borderline personality disorder, which means I'm riddled with self-doubt, and I've lived a life chock-full of adversity. But I've been doing dialectical behavioral therapy for some years now. It's a combination of cognitive behavioral therapy and Zen, developed by Marsha Linehan. I've learned some practical skills along the lines of stress tolerance, interpersonal relations, mindfulness, and emotion management. These DBT skills help me get through the bad patches, and they help me build myself back up when the bad patch is over.

Which of your traits are you most proud of?
Over the last few years, I've gotten better at radical acceptance. That's brought me a great deal of peace and comfort.

What is your personal or professional motto?
All roads in life lead nowhere, so you might as well choose the road that's got the most heart and is the most fun.

What does the world need more of? Less of?
More questions, fewer answers.

What would you tell yourself ten to twenty years ago that you wish you knew then?
I'd say to myself that it's okay to do whatever it takes to make life more worth living—anything at all. The only rule is, *don't be mean*. I'm sure that would've saved me a lot of heartache.

What is your no-fail go-to when you need inspiration or to get out of a creative rut?
I speak with loved ones who know me well enough to help me navigate scary times.

If you were magically given three more hours per day, what would you do with them?
I'd add one hour to work, one hour to play, and one hour to sleep.

What's your favorite thing to come home to after a long day of work?
During my touring seasons, my favorite thing to come home to is a Siberian kitty, purring in my lap.

Name a woman (or women), past or present, whom you admire or look up to.
Harper Lee. She did her work, then she stepped back from it.

What tool, object, or ritual could you not live without in your workday?
My MacBook Pro, connected to the Internet.

> "The biggest lesson I've learned is to prepare for the long haul, the rise and fall, and let neither define your sense of self."

Karen Young

Product Designer,
Entrepreneur
Brooklyn, NY

What did you want to be when you were a child?

I was very attracted to reason and research as a child, and I wanted to be either a lawyer or an anthropologist.

What was the best piece of business advice you were given when you were starting out?

The best piece of advice I was given came well before I knew what an entrepreneur was. When I was seven, my grandmother looked at me very seriously and said in her calm, kind way, "You must learn perseverance." She made me repeat it, spell it, and memorize the definition. She gently explained that sometimes in life you have to carry on in the face of great challenges and adversity. I can't remember exactly what motivated her to say this, but I never forgot it. It was my single greatest preparation for entrepreneurship; everything else I was able to acquire as a skill, but I had been working on perseverance before I even knew what it was.

What is the biggest sacrifice you've made in starting or running your business?

Travel has been the biggest sacrifice in running my business. I've always loved to travel, but growing a business is incredibly demanding of my time. Each stage of growth requires a different level of energy, education, and commitment.

What does success mean to you?

My business has changed what success means to me. When I was younger, my idea of success revolved around tangible things, the things I assumed I'd buy with my hard-earned money. With age and wisdom, I'm more interested in the time and people I enjoy it with. Success now looks like lengthy dinners with friends, laughter, time with family, and as much travel as I can fit into my life. My motto is: Experiences over things.

Name the biggest overall lesson you've learned in running a business.

My good friend tells me at least once a year that it takes ten years to achieve overnight success. I think entrepreneurship can be highly romanticized and polished. Few magazines write about the fortitude required to grow a business, and the real challenges faced beyond the spark of "I can do it!" The biggest lesson I've learned is to prepare for the long haul, the rise and fall, and let neither define your sense of self.

Has learning from a mistake ever led you to success?

For many years I found it difficult to find answers on scaling a business. I would reach out to other entrepreneurs, read as many books and blogs as I could, yet look back at my own business in wonder. Everyone talked about business growth, but no one had details for all the steps in between. The image that comes to my mind is of looking at a smooth glass mountain, with not a foothold in sight, and yet there was a *rumor* that others had climbed it. What tools had they used? How had they approached it? What were the difficult parts? Finding no other answers, I took a leap and scaled my company. I expanded distribution, set up and managed multiple sales teams, and tripled my product line. As a solo entrepreneur I took on what should have been the work of a small team . . . until I crumpled under the weight. It

turns out that the steps in between involve time, patience, a steady pace, skill, funds, and some luck. It involves being nimble and able to quickly adjust to feedback and change. It also involves getting help where and when it's needed to create a thriving business. There were many successes from that experience, including learning how to climb that formidable glass mountain. As a result, I adjusted my business to focus on an improved product, a great story, and growing at a pace that allows me to modify when I need to. I learned to build the business that *I* needed, rather than the one I thought everyone else was building.

In moments of self-doubt or adversity, how do you build yourself back up?
I'm learning to give myself a moment when I need it; whether it's five minutes of meditation in the morning, or half an hour to laugh at a silly TV show. It's a choice to be an entrepreneur, and it's a very immersive and intense experience, but I have to remind myself that while my qualities help me to thrive as an entrepreneur, I'm not defined by what I do.

What quotation or saying inspires and motivates you to be yourself and do what you love?
"What you seek is seeking you." —Rumi.

Which of your traits are you most proud of?
My sheer tenacity.

What tool, object, or ritual could you not live without in your workday?
A blank sheet of paper and a black pen. I can't work well until I see my to-do list in front of me, and crossing things off is incredibly satisfying.

What's the first thing you do every morning to start your day on the right foot?
I have been doing a gratitude list for the last year. Every day I think of three things that I accomplished or experienced the day before that I'm grateful for. The trick is to think about each one in full so that it doesn't become rote; with each thing I'm grateful for, I have to expand upon it to think about *why* I feel grateful. It's a nice way to start the day and a reminder that although some days I feel like I'm barely raising the dust, I am actually moving mountains.

What does the world need more of? Less of?

I think the world needs more authentic, honest, and vulnerable connections. As an individual I think this results in richer relationships, and as a businesswoman I find that the result is a sincere collaboration between my customer and me. Less polish, more authenticity.

> "Looking inside myself rather than to others for innovation or inspiration is the only way I can stay true to myself and stay jazzed about my work."

Christine Schmidt

Artist, Designer
San Francisco, CA

What did you want to be when you were a child?

I always knew I was going to do something with art and design, I just didn't know it would be this. Maybe it won't always be exactly this business, but it's just in me.

What is your favorite thing about your workspace?

My monster worktable. I skip around between different projects. First and best thing I got myself for the new studio.

What is the biggest sacrifice you've made in starting or running your business?

Time for my life outside myself and outside my work. It took motherhood (but it doesn't have to!) to show me that work was soaking up all my waking and nonwaking hours. After I had my daughter I was actually tempted to quit. Luckily, that drive started creeping back in, and I realized that I need this to be whole. Oddly, having

more to do in less time means I work leaner and have less time to doubt myself.

What does success mean to you?

Autonomy. I can take risks I couldn't years ago. Being creative and running a business always requires some compromise, but success to me also means having those two in harmony. The work has to give me as much as it takes away.

Name a fear or professional challenge that keeps you up at night.

Honestly, none. My twin sister, Jessie, died in 2006 when this business was in seed form. As I was slowly piecing myself back together, I built back all the big stuff first, then found I didn't have the energy or need for small unnecessary bits. One of them was fear of things I can't control anyway. This isn't to say I don't worry about whether my sketches will be liked or that the shipment won't arrive in time; just that I know I'll be breathing even if it doesn't.

If you were given $100 million, would you run your business any differently? How so?

I would pay my team like queens and pay off their student loans. All my employees are artists or musicians, and I'd love to be able to support them as much as they support me. Part of me respecting them as employees is honoring them as people who have desires and needs outside of the workplace.

Has learning from a mistake ever led you to success?

A few years into my business, social media was just getting big. Under the guise of business savvy, I thought I had to keep pace with everything happening in my field. I was forcing myself into relationships thinking they were strategic and said yes to things I didn't want to do. I was bending to fit and it was hollowing. Letting go of all that busyness let me refocus and allowed me to make more original work. I also learned that

once something is a trend, its expiration date is set. Looking inside myself rather than to others for innovation or inspiration is the only way I can stay true to myself and stay jazzed about my work.

In moments of self-doubt or adversity, how do you build yourself back up?

I stop thinking and make. I push myself till I get to that effortless place where the otherness between my eyes and brain and hands and paper and paint falls away. This chase is why I chose this work. Running a creative business takes a lot out of me, and I need this part to refill.

What does the world need more of?

Real talk about how the ability to be creative is directly connected to money and politics. If you have the luxury of creative practice, it is your responsibility to exercise it, relish it, and feel gratitude for it. It's also your responsibility as a human to use your vote, your dollars, and/or your time to get other people there. I wonder how many women more deserving than me aren't in this book because they never had the opportunity to use what's in them.

What is your personal or professional motto?

Make something awful, a golden failure. I learn more about my process when something that makes me cringe emerges. If I'm not making mistakes or changing, I'm stagnating. What feels like comforting stillness is really rigor mortis that can trap you. I need movement (even if it's backward) to break it up and grow.

If you were magically given three more hours per day, what would you do with them?

I would spend more time with my daughter and cook more. No recipes or preset expectations—just intuition and stained clothes. That's like all the best parts of my creative work, but I get to eat it afterward.

**Which of your traits are you
most proud of?**

---

*I don't compare
myself to others.
I'm not in
a competition.*

"Be relentless, be ambitious, be excellent."

Roxane Gay

Writer, Professor
West Lafayette, Indiana

What did you want to be when you were a child?
I wanted to be a doctor—a surgeon or an emergency room physician.

What characteristic do you most admire in other creative women?
I admire their tenacity, their capacity for creating beauty and the unexpected forms that beauty takes.

What does success mean to you?
I am still searching for the answer to this question. It scares me because I don't know how to allow myself to feel or appreciate any success I have achieved.

What is your favorite thing about your workspace?
I don't have a singular workspace. Because I travel so much and do such a range of things professionally, my workspace is pretty much wherever I am. Have laptop, will write. My favorite thing, I suppose, is my adaptability, that I am not tied to any one place to create.

If you were given $100 million, would you run your business any differently? How so?
I would write a lot slower. I would really take my time to pick and choose what I wanted to say. It's not that I am indiscriminate now, but I say yes more than I truly want to. I would also create sustainable systems of support for underrepresented writers. Money really does matter when you're trying to make a go of it as a writer. Bills don't get paid on dreams, and so I want to remove that stress from as many underrepresented writers as I can. Just imagine what they would say, freed from the constraints that keep them from writing as much as they would like.

What is the biggest sacrifice you've made in your career/line of work?
Without a doubt, I have sacrificed motherhood.

Has learning from a mistake ever led you to success?
I'm a perfectionist, so when I make a mistake, I really get down on myself. But once I've cleared my head, I look at what I've done wrong and think through ways of fixing that mistake, and I try to find ways of assuring that I won't make that particular mistake again.

Name a fear or professional challenge that keeps you up at night.
I worry that my next essay or story or book won't be good enough, that I will disappoint my fans or that one day I will wake up and I won't find the words to write well.

In moments of self-doubt or adversity, how do you build yourself back up?
I am lucky to have a support system, by way of a person. Certainly, I can build myself back up, but in truth, there is someone who keeps the faith when I falter and I am comfortable admitting that. This idea of the solitary artist is nonsense. My success can be attributed to my hard work and ambition and the support of my person, who is always there, giving me what I need, whether it's a pep talk, a warm smile, or a sharp lecture on getting over myself. In terms of building myself back up, I remind myself that I love writing. I write for me before I write for anyone else.

What is your personal or professional motto?
Be relentless, be ambitious, be excellent.

> "The world looks so different when we remember we are an energy, not an image."

Sarah Neuburger

Artist, Designer
Decatur, GA

What did you want to be when you were a child?

Little Me:
"A teacher."

But really I just loved drawing on the chalkboards after school while waiting to go home. My mom was a kindergarten teacher.

High School Me:
"An accountant."

$1x + 2y =$

I loved the patterns and relationships in numbers. Algebra, especially. I loved that each new problem had a solution I could figure out.

This all changed when one art teacher took me aside and said I was awesome and special. She validated my path.
ONE PERSON changed everything.

What was the best piece of business advice you were given when you were starting out?

The best advice was never hearing it SHOULDN'T or COULDN'T be done.

Name your greatest success (or something you're most proud of) in your business experiences.

THE CONNECTIONS.

Hearing from clients or customers how my work or drawings have been a positive part of their daily lives.

What is your favorite thing about your workspace?

MY DOOR!

I work out of my house, by choice, but I do still love a door for separation. And all the STORAGE!

*Not to scale. *Not really the floor plan, either. Old Library Card Catalog. (This is true.)

If you were magically given three more hours per day, what would you do with them?

TALK TO SOMEONE IN PERSON

In your opinion, what are the top three things someone should consider before starting a business?

ONE- What brings you joy?

TWO- What brings you calm?

THREE- What decision can you live with making?

What is the biggest sacrifice you've made in starting or running your business?

SACRIFICE JAR

Empty. BUT She helps.

Running my own business is made much easier because my wife works and has good health-care plans for us both, and because all expenses are shared. I don't feel I've made any sacrifices but that might look very different if I was going it alone. Before I met my wife and while I was starting my business I lived with my sister...sharing costs again. And aside from financial sacrifices, the opposite has occurred. I feel so fortunate for the experiences I haven't missed because I run my own business.

Name a fear or professional challenge that keeps you up at night.

Wondering if I'm doing "enough" and Taxes.

What does success mean to you?

Success means...
a. Full Trust in the Abundance For Us All.

b. Operating without fear of the scarcity of time, resources, recognition, or Money. There is enough for us all.

The world looks so different when we remember we are an energy, not an image.

What quotation or saying inspires and motivates you to be yourself and do what you love?

THE ONLY LIMITATIONS I HAVE ARE THOSE I SET MYSELF

Name the biggest overall lesson you've learned in running a business.

TRUST IN ME.

YOU MIGHT RELY ON IT

When I follow my intuition I have no regrets and I feel more confident in the path I'm taking.

In moments of self-doubt or adversity, how do you build yourself back up?

BUILD ME UP by CHECKING IN.

I ask myself if what I am doing is making me happy. Would I want to put my energy in a different direction? So far, realigning myself with my goals and priorities does the trick.

Where were you when you came up with the idea for your business or discovered what you wanted to do?

FEMINIST.

In NYC, working at a feminist nonprofit media arts organization realizing that I had just graduated with an MFA, and had a job but was off track. I could ignore it or set it right.

Name the biggest overall lesson you've learned in running a business.

CULTIVATE A KEEN SENSE OF INTUITION AND POSSESS THE COURAGE TO CHANGE COURSE - AT ANY GIVEN POINT.

"The world needs more true connection and time spent with each other."

Gauri Nanda

Product Designer
Brooklyn, NY

What did you want to be when you were a child?

Part of me wishes I had an incredible story of knowing what I wanted to do from a young age. The truth is I had no idea, in part because I was led to believe there were limited options for success—three, to be exact: law, medicine, and engineering. So I did what I thought was expected of me: majored in computer science and eventually worked at Apple.

Then I heard about the Media Lab at MIT and I felt that was where I was meant to be. I reveled in the creativity, the independence I was afforded, and became fearless, attempting the projects I was assigned in new and unconventional ways.

I read a book called *The Design of Everyday Things,* which shifted my worldview. I began to look at so many things as design problems waiting for solutions—anything from objects like alarm clocks that don't do a very good job of getting you out of bed to roads and how their design ultimately impacts the prevalence of car accidents. Technology could be used at times to design things better, and I was someone that could make that happen. More important, I found a passion, realized I could carve out my own path in life and be much more successful and much more fulfilled in doing so.

What is the biggest sacrifice you've made in starting or running your business?

Spending more time than I would like to in front of a screen.

What does success mean to you?

Making a positive impact on the world (however difficult that is to measure), inspiring others, being authentic, and, most important, having meaningful and lasting relationships with people who are authentic too.

Name the biggest overall lesson you've learned in running a business.

You need to have the right people behind you, and there's a lot of trial and error in assembling that. There are a lot of sharks out there and it's difficult to figure out whom you can trust, so don't give them the world. If something feels strange, it probably is. People present themselves as who they want to be, not who they are. Those were a few lessons.

Has learning from a mistake ever led you to success?

When I went to build my new business, Toymail, I thought I knew exactly how to do it because I had bootstrapped a company before and succeeded. But applying that business strategy to Toymail proved ineffectual. After going back to the drawing board (a few times), I learned it is easier to create something with no preconceived notions of how it should be done. Toymail is still very much in the early stages, but in being flexible and changing our strategy, we now have Amazon and Verizon as investors, are closing some major distribution deals, and, most important, have kids as young as two who are able to stay connected to those they love, on their own, for the first time in their lives, without being put in front of a screen. We are building healthy uses of technology for kids, and believe very strongly in this mission.

In moments of self-doubt or adversity, how do you build yourself back up?

I call my best friend. I also have a "remember" list, things that resonate with me, things like "most problems are blessings in disguise" and "it's a choice to enjoy this adventure and not get caught up in its problems."

What does the world need more of?

The world needs more true connection and time spent with each other.

Which of your traits are you most proud of?

Empathy.

What is your personal or professional motto?

I actually think Nike got it right when they said, "Just do it." My best friend laughs at me whenever I utter this slogan, but I see a lot of people who want to change something yet default to getting stuck in their thoughts.

What tool, object, or ritual could you not live without in your workday?

I clean up. I can be more focused and precise when the objects around me are well ordered. I once read a quote: "One of life's greatest joys is putting an object back in its right place." I thought that was both true and amusing.

What's the first thing you do every morning to start your day on the right foot?

I eat two breakfasts. One sweet and one savory.

"Success in business is seeing how badly you can fail and still love yourself."

Mary Going

Fashion Designer
Berkeley, CA

What was the best piece of business advice you were given when you were starting out?

My mentor, Michael Bush, always says, "Hire slow, fire fast." That is great advice that I haven't always followed, but when I do, it serves me beautifully.

What is your favorite thing about your workspace?

Our workspace at Saint Harridan is full of scrappy creativity. I love the way we "hack" design. For example, when we moved into our space, the walls were in very rough shape, and we were quoted $6,000 to smooth and paint them. Pinterest helped us find a paper bag and Elmer's glue solution, and we hired a friend/customer to do the work for a fraction of the original quote. Plus, it looks better than a flat paint job would have looked. Similarly, we used old doors to create our dressing rooms. The effect is much more interesting than built walls, and again, the cost was minimal.

What does success mean to you?

Success in business is seeing how badly you can fail and still love yourself.

What is your personal or professional motto?

You have to be willing to be bad at it in order to get good at it.

What resources would you recommend to someone starting a creative business?

The most important resource is other entrepreneurs. Don't ask them generic "How did you do that?" questions. Rather, ask them specific, thoughtful questions. Most will be happy to help another entrepreneur or someone considering the path.

Name the biggest overall lesson you've learned in running a business.

The biggest lesson is that running a business is not about instincts, but about things you can and must learn. I have an MBA, but I would argue that's not the source of the best education. I used to tell my kids they absolutely had to go to college. Now I wonder if they wouldn't be better off with the library, YouTube, and Khan Academy. And, of course, with a try/fail/try again attitude.

Has learning from a mistake ever led you to success?

I have made lots of mistakes, and I hope I've learned from all of them. One in particular is that I hired someone because she is smart and works hard, and then gave her a huge project—one that I didn't even know how to do myself—and assumed she could figure it out. She couldn't but was embarrassed about that and didn't let me know, so it wasn't until things started falling through the cracks that I realized she wasn't doing a good job. So, the first mistake was setting unrealistic expectations and having no oversight. The second mistake was getting angry when the facade crumbled, revealing months' worth of mess. Getting angry did nothing for the problem and damaged our relationship. It took a long time to recover from that mistake—both because of the underlying mess and because of the damage to the relationship. The success, though, is that I learned I can't just dump projects on anyone—no matter how smart or skilled. More important, I had to learn to control my reactions to anger. Ultimately, I am a better leader because of this failure, but I'm sorry that I had to learn that on a live person.

In your opinion, what should someone consider before starting a business?

People often go into business because they love something: baking pies, building furniture, designing clothes. The reality of being a business owner is that your occupation is not Pie Maker, Furniture Builder, or Clothing Designer. Your occupation is Entrepreneur. If you don't love business, you will not love your job.

What's the first thing you do every morning to start your day on the right foot?

Julia Cameron's "Morning Pages" (from *The Artist's Way*). I was in a motorcycle accident years ago and can no longer do longhand writing, so I use a website called 750words.com.

Name a woman (or women), past or present, whom you admire or look up to.

I am in awe of Anna Deavere Smith, whose relationship with her craft is incredibly intense and skilled. I admire the way she uses that craft to influence public conversations and create positive change.

If you were magically given three more hours per day, what would you do with them?

Knowing me, I would probably work, but I might also get more sleep!

"My brain is wired to find the humor in every situation."

Desiree Akhavan

Writer, Actor,
Filmmaker, Director
London, England

What did you want to be when you were a child?

I knew I wanted to tell stories, and I started writing sketches and plays around the age of nine. That said, I put a lot of effort into studying and trying to become a normal, functioning, "book smart" human being, with a stable job. But the level of mediocrity I brought to the table was astonishing. I am not capable of doing any other job. So far, I've been the world's worst receptionist, salesperson, live-in nanny, and research assistant.

What characteristic do you most admire in other creative women?

All creative people I know are huge fans of things and love discovering great art (whether it be music, TV, film, fine art, puppetry—seriously, whatever).

What does success mean to you?

The ability to support yourself through your work without compromising on vision or values.

Has learning from a mistake ever led you to success?

The first few short films I made were to please everyone *but* me. I kept trying to anticipate what Sundance would like to program or what the professors in my film program would appreciate. Every choice I made was deeply layered with "Will people like this?" As a result, I spent a year making a short film that lacked all the humor and risk that make me who I am, and for that reason it did nothing. I shot on film because that's what other people kept saying a "serious filmmaker" was supposed to do and wasted money I didn't have. I sent it to thirty film festivals and was rejected almost everywhere.

After that experience I cocreated a web series called *The Slope* for no money with zero thought as to how it would be perceived or what it should be modeled after, because at that time there weren't many web series out there to compare it to. It was all about following my taste and instincts and not worrying about the results. The show was well received and brought me to the next level in my career.

Which of your traits are you most proud of?

My brain is wired to find the humor in every situation.

What does the world need more of? Less of?

More risk taking, less ego.

In moments of self-doubt or adversity, how do you build yourself back up?

I love reading interviews where filmmakers speak openly about failure. There's a fantastic book I've read about ten times called *My First Movie*, where filmmakers talk very candidly about the process of making their first films. Almost everyone fails before they succeed. And only the delusional people manage to get through life without feeling like a huge loser and/or fake.

What would you tell yourself ten to twenty years ago that you wish you knew then?

Everything is going to be fine. You're talented and attractive enough. For both love and success. You don't have to trick people into believing in you. It will come but you need patience, 'cause it's not coming *for a long-ass time*.

What is your no-fail go-to when you need inspiration or to get out of a creative rut?

Talking with my producing partner, Ceci, and/or watching something brilliant.

"Throw hesitation and insecurity out the window."

Jasmine Wright

Tattoo Artist
San Diego, CA

What did you want to be when you were a child?

When I was a kid, the only career I ever remember feeling any sort of inclination toward was being a masseuse, which I admit was due to watching too many episodes of *Friends* and having Phoebe as a favorite character. I also briefly believed I wanted to be a lawyer, but I let that go as soon as I realized the cost, length, and weight of law school. I don't think I'm wired for that kind of structured environment.

What characteristic do you most admire in other creative women?

The fearlessness it requires to be your own architect, to have a vision for your life plan no matter how obscure, and to take it all by the horns and make it yours.

What is your favorite thing about your workspace?

I surround myself with several pieces of art from close friends and individuals I admire and who keep me inspired. Their art serves as a constant reminder that they're also following this weird path of doing what they do to stay happy, like I am.

What is the biggest sacrifice you've made in your career/line of work?

Over the past few years, the tattoo world has been gaining popularity due to several TV shows. This has led to a giant misconception among the general public that being a tattoo artist is this "rock star" career, where you'll land on TV and make tons of money. Let me be the one to break it to them that it's not. People don't realize that this career path is heavily laden with deep traditions, and dues to be paid, and an unimaginably huge amount of sacrifice and effort to be put in if you want to do it right.

Name a fear or professional challenge that keeps you up at night.

A consistent worry of mine is maintaining the ability to stay motivated and inspired from within. This craft is such a unique, internally driven skill, and only I can keep my passion and interest alive. I worry about being able to keep up with the progression of my peers, and keeping myself on a continuously upward path, pushing my work to its personal best version.

What would you tell yourself ten to twenty years ago that you wish you knew then?

Throw hesitation and insecurity out the window.

What is your no-fail go-to when you need inspiration or to get out of a creative rut?

Travel has been my most important tool for escaping creative ruts. In the last five years, I've seen thirteen countries and forty of the fifty states.

What tool, object, or ritual could you not live without in your workday?

Music. I can't begin to explain how much of a difference the daily sound track can make in my workday. I've also found this subject to be the most common battle among coworkers. But my iPod is like gold to me: it sets my pace and mood for whatever project I have in front of me, and it changes between each client/tattoo. It's become a very important ritual to select an appropriate playlist for my day. It has nothing to do with tattooing, but has *everything* to do with it as well.

> "I love that over the years, so many clients have become great friends."

Lisa Folawiyo

Fashion Designer
Lagos, Nigeria

What did you want to be when you were a child?

I wanted to be one of two things: a lawyer or a writer. With much persuasion from my parents, I went with law.

What was the best piece of business advice you were given when you were starting out?

Not long after Jewel by Lisa was established, my sister-in-law, who had dabbled in designing and tailoring in previous years, said to me, "Never say no. Whenever an opportunity comes, take it; difficult or easy, say you can do it. You will make your mistakes—learn from your lessons." This still serves me well. Of course, a few years on, I've learned to be more discerning and can detect a really bad opportunity a mile away. But even with that, I say more yeses than nos and have passed this piece of advice on to my team.

What is your favorite thing about your workspace?

The abundance of rich color and print against the white walls and minimal decor. Every time I walk into the work studio, I feel a rush of excitement bursting out of a cool, serene space. I absolutely love it. It depicts who we are: a great amount of seriousness with equal amounts of fun and youthful exuberance.

What is the biggest sacrifice you've made in starting or running your business?

I had my daughter the year before I started the label, and my son not too long after. It was quite hard to juggle two really young children with a new business. As with everything, it all balanced out, and although I continue to make sacrifices, it's not as difficult to prioritize these days.

Which of your traits are you most proud of?

Patience.

What tool, object, or ritual could you not live without in your workday?

My ritual would be prayer. Tool would be my iPhone. And of course some Instagramming is necessary.

Name a woman (or women), past or present, whom you admire or look up to.

Without any hesitation, it would be my mum. A young Trinidadian woman marrying a charming Nigerian in London, then moving to Nigeria, which she knew nothing about, and creating a wonderful life for her family. She worked her way to the top of the civil service ladder and achieved such great success. Even in retirement, she continues to pursue her dreams and goals. She is a Wonder Woman. She is amazing. If I can be half the woman she is, I'll be good.

What does the world need more of? Less of?

The world needs more love and less ignorance.

Has learning from a mistake ever led you to success?

I must say that creating the best customer experiences for our clients has seen us have a high rate of return clients who come not only to buy but sometimes just for that experience. I love that over the years, so many clients have become good friends.

> "The world could always use more people who are interested in lifting up others, not only themselves."

Christy Turlington Burns

Activist, Model
New York, NY

What did you want to be when you were a child?
I started working as a model when I was still a child, so I didn't have too much time to dream, but I did know I wanted to travel. Some other possibilities were an architect, a writer, or a pilot.

What was the best piece of business advice you were given when you were starting out?
Some great advice I received early on was to take extra time for myself to travel when in another country or city for work, and to always seek out friends of friends or family when abroad to get a better perspective on a place and then continue to nurture those relationships.

What does success mean to you?
Success to me is when I am feeling purposeful, authentic, and of service to others.

What is the biggest sacrifice you've made in starting or running your business?
I nearly sacrificed my relationship with my husband before we got married when I had my first businesses years ago. I learned that family must come first, and when I started Every Mother Counts I vowed not to let it take over my life.

What quotation or saying inspires and motivates you to be yourself and do what you love?
"The best way to find yourself is to lose yourself in the service of others." —attributed to Gandhi

At what point in your life did you first learn about your field of work? What called you to it?
I started advocating for health and wellness after losing my dad to lung cancer in 1997. I discovered that it was not only incredibly healing to share his story of addiction to tobacco and my own story about the premature loss of a father with others, but that it also actually helped others take steps to improve their own health for themselves and their loved ones. I became a global maternal health-care advocate the day I became a mom. I experienced a childbirth-related complication after delivering my daughter, Grace, in 2003 and learned after I recovered that hundreds of thousands of girls and women die each year bringing life into the world. That was shocking to learn, especially since I had endured and survived this experience that is so celebrated yet also taken for granted. I started Every Mother Counts as a campaign to make timely and appropriate maternal health care accessible to every mother.

Name your greatest success (or something you're most proud of) in your business experiences.
I'm proud that this life-changing experience has brought me closer to so many girls and women, and that our mission is inspiring others to work together to impact the lives of people they don't already know.

What does the world need more of?
The world could always use more people who are interested in lifting up others, not only themselves.

"Being an artist means you are always working."

Shizu Saldamando

Artist
Los Angeles, CA

What did you want to be when you were a child?

I think I wanted to be the next Kristi Yamaguchi. But over time I realized I had a better chance at becoming a professional artist. As far back as I can remember, my mom took me to work with her since she could not afford day care. I would sit in a corner of her office and draw to entertain myself, so from a very early age I was drawing and developing that skill. Around my neighborhood back then, there was a really large, active Chicano art scene that was a huge influence on me, providing inspiration for what I could do with that creativity. When I graduated from high school, I got into UCLA's art school and went from there.

What is the biggest sacrifice you've made in starting or running your business?

Being an artist means you are always working. You never have set hours or can ever really take a vacation from it. I am always on the lookout for things that inspire me and could turn into possible art projects. You work nights, early mornings, sometimes forgetting to eat just to finish what you set out in your head to create. It's a constant process that is really difficult to take a break from.

What does success mean to you?

Success to me is being psychologically healthy, happy, and secure with who you are as a person regardless of income, position, or title.

Name a fear or professional challenge that keeps you up at night.

Working and living in East L.A., I worry about how the current systems of capitalism are intrinsically white supremacist and misogynist and how I might be contributing to that. It is a large issue that I see manifested daily through casual language and aggressions against certain people. I see it happen nationally, and it does keep me up at night. I worry about our future as a country and how I am countering or contributing to the problem as an artist. I am constantly thinking about becoming redundant or unknowingly upholding current repressive structures.

If you were given $100 million, would you run your business any differently? How so?

Yes. I think I would try to fund art programs in public schools where the property values are low. I think studying art is such a valuable staple in creating critical thinkers who can challenge media and societal norms.

Name the biggest overall lesson you've learned in running a business.

As an artist, I've learned it is very important to find a day job that can contribute to your craft and inform your projects, not take away from them. After working as an artist's assistant for a while after graduate school, I wondered how else I could serve myself and make money. Tattooing seemed like the logical answer since I have the drawing skills, and it's really helped me reconnect with people who inspired me to create in the first place. It's become a very therapeutic process and a little spiritual in the intimacy and trauma that is both released and created.

Name your greatest success (or something you're most proud of) in your business experiences.

Being able to exhibit at the Venice Biennale, LACMA, and the Smithsonian while working at a tattoo shop in East L.A. has been really awesome. Being able to code switch not only in verbal language but also artistically is something I'm really proud of.

"My self-worth is separate from my creative work and any response it may or may not elicit."

Thao Nguyen
Musician, Songwriter
San Francisco, CA

What did you want to be when you were a child?

I wanted to be an actor, writer, and musician, and appear on *Oprah*, all at once.

What characteristic do you most admire in other creative women?

I admire their fire and their empathy, their devotion to what they make and the consistent return to work, no matter the perceived success or failure. I admire these things because I believe them to be what is most important about creativity, and at my best, they are what I strive most to meet and inhabit.

What does success mean to you?

Making/performing music as my full-time job, compromising only within my bounds of rational compromise, access to making things with people I admire, making enough money to not stress about money, recognizing how lucky I am to have the freedom to pursue whatever I will, and showing and sharing that gratitude.

What is the biggest sacrifice you've made in your career/line of work?

The biggest and most grim sacrifices I've made are all to do with being present for many of the important life events (big and small) of the people I love. Those closest to me have had to make this sacrifice as well, and it is something that makes me consistently sad about my job. I can't tell you how many weddings and birthdays and dinners and births and afternoons in the park and whatever I've missed. It can be hard when people you love get used to you being away.

Has learning from a mistake ever led you to success?

My greatest professional mistake has been complacency. At the time in question I was dissatisfied and depressed with my work and my professional progress in general. I just sank into a sort of lulling lament. I had to learn that complacency got me into my mental mess, and complacency kept me there, and the only thing to do was shut up and get it together. Also, a huge thing I had to learn was not to compare my career to the careers of others. Compare and despair. It's helpful to take note of other people's success and funnel it into motivation, using their successes as examples and benchmarks.

In moments of self-doubt or adversity, how do you build yourself back up?

I remember that my self-worth is separate from my creative work and any response it may or may not elicit. I remember all the times I've conflated the two and the misery that ensued. I remember that there is a lot of good and terrible shit happening that is so much bigger than what I am doing and that I am so lucky to be doing this for my living. And if I operate under the auspices and shade of sincere gratitude and respect, then everything is okay, I get over myself, and I get back to work.

What inspires and motivates you to be yourself and do what you love?

I think of all the friends I visit every six weeks through the California Coalition for Women Prisoners who are serving decades/life sentences without parole, and they ground me and inspire me to live in action and joy.

"Be you and not another."

Olimpia Zagnoli

Illustrator
Milan, Italy

What did you want to be when you were a child?
At first I wanted to be an architect and build tree houses, then an engineer and build strange cars like the Banana Car, to park on curves, then I got a pencil case with an astronaut pattern on it and I wanted to become an astronaut.

What characteristic do you most admire in other creative women?
They don't talk much about their work—they work.

Has learning from a mistake ever led you to success?
I had to learn a lot in the financial department. I spent years not getting paid, forgetting to send invoices, not keeping all my receipts just because I considered it boring. I had this feeling that as long as I was having fun doing this job, everything would turn out just fine. Well, I was stupid. Now I understand that my instinct was good, but it has to be paired with discipline and care.

In moments of self-doubt or adversity, how do you build yourself back up?
I believe in myself, and I have a feeling I will do good things in the future. This doesn't mean I don't have moments of self-criticism—I often do—but I consider them constructive rather than discouraging.

What quotation or saying inspires and motivates you to be yourself and do what you love?
"The life of the creative man is led, directed and controlled by boredom. Avoiding boredom is one of our most important purposes." —Saul Steinberg

What is your personal or professional motto?
Be you and not another.

What does the world need more of? Less of?
More education. Less everything that comes from the lack of education.

What would you tell yourself ten to twenty years ago that you wish you knew then?
Gummy bears are not fruit, therapy can be interesting, don't judge people by their shoes.

What is your no-fail go-to when you need inspiration or to get out of a creative rut?
Museums and bookstores. I could spend hours in a bookstore looking at book covers or reading about how to knit clouds.

What's your favorite thing to come home to after a long day of work?
Boyfriend, bare feet, breadsticks, bed.

Name a woman (or women), past or present, whom you admire or look up to.
Margherita Hack was an Italian astrophysicist born in 1922. She was vegetarian, unconsciously feminist, and openly against religion, which in a country like Italy are still unusual things.

> "I try to remind myself that every mistake made is a lesson learned and a step toward improving, and that perseverance is my greatest asset."

Hana Getachew

Textile Designer
Brooklyn, NY

What did you want to be when you were a child?

From the time I was very young I wanted to be a visual artist, like a painter or an illustrator. I spent much of my free time drawing and painting. Unlike a lot of architects I know, who knew what their calling was at a young age, very few people I've met in interiors, furniture, and textile design started out knowing that's what they wanted to do. I believe it's because architecture is an ancient, well-established, and revered field, while other parts of the industry are less accessible to the general population. Design and design-thinking are much more part of the American vocabulary now than they were when I was a student. In the end, I love being a designer and couldn't imagine doing anything else.

What was the best piece of business advice you were given when you were starting out?

"Just start! Even if you're only 60 percent there, just start." If I hadn't heard this, I'd probably still be planning my launch. I'm not a perfectionist, but I definitely like to be prepared and to always feel like I've given my work as much thought and effort as possible.

What is your favorite thing about your workspace?

The natural light, hands down. It's why my husband and I chose this apartment and why I chose the room (over his futile protests) as my workspace. He's a writer and works from home, and because I worked in an architecture firm for much of our relationship, he usually got to pick which space in all of our previous apartments he wanted for his office. Not this time. We decided to move out of our last place just as I was starting my business, which meant that for the first time, we would both be working from home. When we first saw our current apartment, and especially the room off the backyard, I knew I had found my headquarters. My studio space faces south and is the brightest room in the house. All that light brings the space to life and makes it easy to work and be creative. My interior design career was focused on workplace design, and I know how critical access to natural light is in fostering productivity, health, and well-being. I'm so fortunate to have this space.

What is the biggest sacrifice you've made in starting or running your business?

Leaving an office environment has been a bit of a sacrifice. The main thing I miss is collaborating with other designers and getting feedback from clients. Any design process is always more successful as a collaboration, so at times it's difficult to work on my own. But I am constantly sending new work to friends and fellow designers to re-create that experience and get another perspective.

What does success mean to you?

Whether it's the financial support that allows our partner artisans to grow their businesses and realize their dreams, the pride the Ethiopian community feels in seeing our products, our customers learning about Ethiopian culture through the brand, or inspiring a future entrepreneur, impacting people in a positive way is the standard by which I'll judge our success.

If you were given $100 million, would you run your business any differently? How so?

Yes! I'd have a team. I'd bring in a chief financial officer and a chief marketing officer and scale up the business with dedicated production and design teams. I also think a lot about having my own weaving studio in Ethiopia. A windfall of capital would allow me to experiment more with new products and techniques. It would also allow me to have a greater impact in Ethiopia. But as wonderful as having loads of cash sounds, it's also a huge responsibility, and I would want to be adequately prepared for an undertaking of that scale.

Name the biggest overall lesson you've learned in running a business.

Patience and agility. I've really had to learn to go with the flow. I am a huge planner, but things often don't go according to plan. Sometimes a shipment gets stuck in customs, or the labels come in the wrong size, or they run out of medium gray yarn in all of Addis Ababa (this really happened). I have to be prepared to take the givens of any scenario, work with what I've got, and avoid having a meltdown!

In moments of self-doubt or adversity, how do you build yourself back up?

This is something I am still trying to navigate. I always try to step back and see the current moment as just that, a moment that will soon pass. I try to remind myself that every mistake made is a lesson learned and a step toward improving, and that perseverance is my greatest asset. I've also been known to play my "girl power" playlist incredibly loudly. Beyoncé reminding me who runs the world is a great morale booster.

In your opinion, what are the top three things someone should consider before starting a business?

1. Vision—do you have a clear idea of what your business is, whom it serves, and the value it offers those clients? Define it until every detail is clear in your mind. Also, determine how you will define success.

2. Team—even if you are planning to go it alone, identify two or three go-to people who can help you build your business. You will need more help than you think!

3. Financial plan—even if you don't create a full business plan, create a business narrative, and outline your budget for at least the first year. Determine what your ceiling is for how much of your own money you're willing to invest in your business in case you go over what you've originally budgeted for, which you will.

Nobody tells you this, but it's impossible to start a business *and* support yourself unless you (a) continue working full- or part-time, (b) have a financial support system or other income-generating scenario (e.g., property) in place, or (c) are independently wealthy.

I would have had a much tougher time starting Bolé Road Textiles if my husband weren't around to keep the lights on. The rest was my savings.

What is your no-fail go-to when you need inspiration or to get out of a creative rut?

I actually have the exact opposite problem. I usually have way too many ideas, more than I could possibly explore in a reasonable time frame. I think both problems—no ideas and too many ideas—can be paralyzing. Constantly having to evaluate and edit for the best result is what great designers do. When working on interiors projects, I often would have ten options I explored on my own before narrowing those down to a few to show the client. I admire designers who are more decisive and have an inherent sense of the best option. I need to hone that skill. Luckily, textile design lends itself to iterating more than interior design does. If I want to have ten colorways and ten variations on a pattern, I can!

dwell in possibility

> "The craft of stand-up is failing onstage, evaluating why you failed, and then preventing that in the future. It puts a positive value on failure—a skill that benefits any businessperson."

Cameron Esposito

Comedian, Actor
Los Angeles, CA

What did you want to be when you were a child?
A priest.

What does success mean to you?
A giant billboard in Times Square with my face on it.

What is your favorite thing about your workspace?
The commute. My desk is at the foot of my bed.

If you were given $100 million, would you run your business any differently? How so?
I'd take a damn vacation. Downtime fuels good, innovative work, but it's difficult to leave space for it when you're self-employed and don't work traditional hours. Any time can be work time. I'd like to think that if I had that big a pile of money,

119

I'd hire on some help and recharge a bit, but I also know myself and I'd probably work the same hours but wear slightly nicer boots.

What is the biggest sacrifice you've made in your career/line of work?
Any sort of normalcy/dependability in schedule and income.

Has learning from a mistake ever led you to success?
The craft of stand-up is failing onstage, evaluating why you failed, and then preventing that particular failure in the future. It's a great craft to hone because it puts a positive value on failure—a skill that benefits any businessperson.

Name a fear or professional challenge that keeps you up at night.
I don't have anything really tangible that says I have "made it" in comedy—just my name and my memories and the things marked on my calendar. I worry that if I stop for a moment, everything I have created will go away.

In moments of self-doubt or adversity, how do you build yourself back up?
I listen to Queen.

Which of your traits are you most proud of?
Fortitude. I learned from my dad, a small-business owner, and my mom, who managed our household when I was young and then went back to work, that nothing in life comes easy. The first decade of a career in comedy is built on constant rejection, which is great practice for the larger rejections that come with greater success. It's a career made in inches and I can't believe I made it through.

What would you tell yourself ten to twenty years ago that you wish you knew then?
There is no formula for success—you just begin and then you continue. I'm often asked how to have a career in stand-up and the answer is confoundingly simple: Do the work. Over and over again, just do the work. After you build the courage to get onstage that first time, it's all about repetition.

What's the hardest thing about being your own boss that isn't obvious?
Loneliness. I'm not only my own boss; I'm also the sole employee of my business. I work with a wonderful team of people, and often collaborate with my fiancée, whom I trust completely and am lucky enough to be able to speak with about all career concerns and issues, but at the end of the day, it's just me.

Where were you when you came up with the idea for your business or discovered what you wanted to do?
I was in the den at my parents' house. I'd just moved back to my hometown, Chicago, from Boston and was living with my parents and preparing to attend grad school for social work when I realized I wanted to do comedy full-time. I still attended about six months of grad school just to make sure, and yes, turns out I didn't want to be a social worker.

What is your no-fail go-to when you need inspiration or to get out of a creative rut?
Exercise. I live at the base of a mountain in Los Angeles and try to get up there every day to hike, to clear my head of any cobwebs and step outside the necessary self-focus that comes with being self-employed, and remember the vastness and variety of the world.

What's the first thing you do every morning to start your day on the right foot?
Begin answering e-mails immediately. Is that not healthy?

Name a woman (or women), past or present, whom you admire or look up to.
I really appreciate and love what fellow comic Maria Bamford has done with her talent and career. She basically created an entirely new genre of stand-up—she does highly personal material focused on the small details and gorgeously risky in delivery. She was the first touring comic I opened for on the road, and the way she was able to be utterly herself onstage made a headlining career seem both out of reach (because I couldn't imagine getting to that level of honesty) and accessible (because I knew it would be rewarding to try).

What characteristic do you most admire in other creative women?

I love a proud woman, a gal who refuses to put herself last or minimize her achievements.

"Go where you want to grow."

Shadi Petosky

Writer, Executive Producer, Showrunner
Los Angeles, CA

What is the biggest sacrifice you've made in starting or running your business?

I'm not sure I've given up anything that was important to me. I didn't go to college, I have an autoimmune disorder, and then I transitioned fifteen years ago, so I had a hard time getting a job in the agency/design world. Starting my own studio, Puny Entertainment, was my only option if I wanted to do creative work. I didn't notice any sacrifice—the world just told me what to do with one thousand microaggressions.

What does success mean to you?

Making an idea real is the only success that matters to me. I'd like to have my own show, but I don't feel unsuccessful without one if I can keep doing pilots and other little things. Collaborating well feels like success.

Has learning from a mistake ever led you to success?

I can't think of specific examples because it's so routine. I make mistakes all the time. I apologize constantly. It's the price of figuring things out.

Name a fear or professional challenge that keeps you up at night.

I have generalized anxiety, so anything can keep me up, but it usually has to do with the end of a project. When this ends, will I ever work again? Will I have to trade down, take marketing work I hate? Will I have a new script ready at the moment I meet the person who can buy it? I now know fear and anxiety aren't worthwhile, so I work on getting to sleep.

In moments of self-doubt or adversity, how do you build yourself back up?

I'm way into "mindfulness," even though I make fun of it, and go to therapy two to three days a week. I read self-help books and have all these little tricks to not be fatalistic. Like imagining tree branches growing through any negative scene playing in my head, from *The Nerdist Way*.

At what point in your life did you first learn about your field of work? What called you to it?

I did really well in high school math and was into computers. At twenty, I was working at a restaurant with these high school kids who were into computers and phone phreaking. They loaned me a computer and I realized I had a knack for programming. I ended up with a commercial space next to Vincent Stall, an amazing cartoonist and an art director at a large agency. He hired me to program Flash sites and I learned design with him sitting over my shoulder, telling me to kern and how to make things pixel perfect.

Name your greatest success (or something you're most proud of) in your business experiences.

That's *Yo Gabba Gabba!* for sure. Robert Schneider of the Apples in Stereo said, "Kids are the ultimate creative scene. They're dancing, painting, singing, drawing more than anyone." What was happening around *Yo Gabba Gabba!* felt like the creative center of the universe. Everyone was involved or wanted to be. All the bands, all the comics and actors, all the artists and designers, and the audience appreciated it so much. We'd make a short video or a game and get all this fan art. That first tour opening night, being

with thousands of dancing toddlers—I don't know if I'll feel that again. We did sixty-something episodes and through two hundred accidents on the business side, it lived fast, died young. Everyone who worked on that show was like, "What do we do now?"

What resources would you recommend to someone starting a creative business?

Read everything you can about starting a business and pitching. Go to the library and get anything about it. There isn't a magic book for everyone, so you kind of have to sift through a lot. Just the act of reading business or inspirational books can put you into a good mind-set.

Knowing what you know now, what would you have done differently when you were first starting out?

I would have moved to Los Angeles right away. As a trans person, I was terrified for my safety. When I saw Ricki Lake in *Where the Day Takes You*, I *knew* her life was my future. I'd like to have had less fear overall, but even today location matters. Go where you want to grow.

What does the world need more of? Less of?

More listening. More learning than dropping your hot take. More intersectionality. Less consumption; we don't need to binge eat animals.

Which of your traits are you most proud of?

I'm autodidactic and can learn things on my own. I have that nerdy brain that will focus, and then time stops. It can focus on the wrong things, like binge watching TV or an addicting mobile game, but when I use that quality in the right way, it works for me.

What is your personal or professional motto?

Get in over your head. It's Ira Glass's, but I took it. "Get in over your head and steal from Ira Glass."

What tool, object, or ritual could you not live without in your workday?

Flair pens. Graph paper. A shower and a nap.

Name a woman (or women), past or present, whom you admire or look up to.

Almost all the people I admire are women. I haven't followed her in years but if I have to name *one* woman, I'd give so much credit and admiration to Ani DiFranco. Much of my personality and politics came from going to her shows and listening to her, almost exclusively, from age nineteen to twenty-four. She epitomizes empathy, spirit, business autonomy, a more liberal feminism, sexual freedom, and the value of travel.

What is your no-fail go-to when you need inspiration or to get out of a creative rut?

Work through it. *Maybe* go for a walk but not near stores or errands. "Looking for inspiration" is the kiss of death for me.

> "The fact that I know I will survive and keep getting back up gets me through any rough patch."

Amina Mucciolo

Artist, Designer
Los Angeles, CA

What did you want to be when you were a child?

Other than that brief period when I wanted to be Janet Jackson, I have wanted to be a writer since I was about five years old.

What is your favorite thing about your workspace?

My favorite thing about our studio is the amazing natural light. When all the windows are open, it often feels like we're floating through the sky. It's pretty dreamy.

What does success mean to you?

Success for me means loving and accepting myself and using my creativity to have a positive effect on the world around me.

Name the biggest overall lesson you've learned in running a business.

Know when to ask for or find help. Studio Mucci has experienced major growth in various stages and each time, to my own detriment, I waited until the last possible minute to ask for help. Help in the form of advice from lawyers or accountants. Help from friends and family, as well as hiring people to meet the needs of the business.

It's still hard. I think it goes along with the territory of transitioning from artist to entrepreneur, but I'm totally getting better at recognizing the needs of the business, especially when they are ones that I simply can't fulfill alone.

In moments of self-doubt or adversity, how do you build yourself back up?

It's not always easy, but one of my greatest qualities is definitely resilience. I have survived so much in my personal life—depression, bulimia, poverty—that I feel like I can handle anything. Sure, I have my moments when I need to cry in a bathroom or times when I feel completely insecure. But the fact that I know I will survive and keep getting back up gets me through any rough patch.

Knowing what you know now, what would you have done differently when you were first starting out?

I think I would have taken myself seriously a lot sooner. I didn't really have any business experience before this, and when I started selling my designs and orders started to quickly roll in, I had no idea what I was doing. I thought it was okay to wing it and figure things out as I went. I've learned that even a little bit of preparation and research goes a long way in life and especially in business.

Which of your traits are you most proud of?

That I allow myself to be vulnerable. That alone has helped me to live a life I never dreamed was possible.

What's your favorite thing to come home to after a long day of work?

Silence. We really don't get enough of it in this world. I so look forward to those moments of just pure silence, even if it's just for ten minutes.

"Be nice to people. Stay humble. Give back."

Justina Blakeney

Designer, Artist, Author
Los Angeles, CA

What did you want to be when you were a child?

When I was a child, I wanted to be a trapeze artist and join the circus. When I was in middle school, I wanted to be an art teacher. In my high school years, I toyed with the idea of being a newscaster, or a diplomat, then I finally settled on folksinger.

What was the best piece of business advice you were given when you were starting out? (Or a piece of advice you're glad you ignored?)

Take a deep breath, then ask for double.

Piece I ignored: When I started blogging in 2009, I had several people tell me that blogging was dead and not to waste my time starting a blog. I was told that the blogs that were already big would stay popular but it was too late to grow a blog into a business. I ended up forging ahead with my blog because I loved doing it—in the end, it has paid off.

Name a fear or professional challenge that keeps you up at night.

The money stuff is stressful. It has taken me many years to think of myself as a businessperson, and I still struggle with it. I often feel like I need to hire a business consultant or manager to deal with the "money stuff" because I don't know what I'm doing. What I'm slowly learning, however, is that

I know better than anyone what is good for my business—I also care more than anyone else what happens to my business and therefore am learning to trust my gut and ask lots of questions.

Name a woman (or women), past or present, whom you admire or look up to.

Frida Kahlo: impeccable grace, deep talent, brave, bold, vulnerable.

Has learning from a mistake ever led you to success?

After months of pitches and meetings, I landed a licensing deal with a very large and wonderful retailer to design a collection of small objects for them. It was very exciting but also stressful, as it was my first collection of this nature and I was unfamiliar with the sampling and manufacturing process. I spent months developing the collection, meticulously creating technical sheets and specifications for the factories—which is not my forte. There was a ton of back-and-forth with the buyers, and finally after a lot of compromises the collection was complete. When the samples came back from the factory months later, they looked nothing like my original vision. I thought I would have the opportunity to modify the samples for a second round, but instead the retailer decided to drop the collection. I actually cried real tears when my agent broke the news. What made matters worse was that in my contract, I was to receive payment after purchase orders were made—and since the orders were never placed, I never got paid. It was very difficult to pick myself up after that experience. Since then I've had several new partners and have learned a lot about sampling and manufacturing. After that experience I've learned to play to my strengths—I've hired a technical designer to create specs and tech packs so that I can focus on the creative and stay in close communication with my partners. I am also very careful about contracts—I get advances and make sure that I'm covered for my hours of work regardless of whether the items end up in stores.

What quotation or saying inspires and motivates you to be yourself and do what you love?

"If you can walk, you can dance. If you can talk, you can sing." —African proverb

Name your greatest success (or something you're most proud of) in your business experiences.

My book, *The New Bohemians*, just made the *New York Times* bestseller list. I never in a million years thought I'd be a *New York Times* bestselling author. It's very trippy and extremely gratifying. Also it's amazing to hear (and see) how people incorporate my ideas into their homes to live more colorful and fantastic lives!

In your opinion, what are the top three things someone should consider before starting a business?

1. If you crave stability, being a business owner is probably not the best idea.
2. You must be extraordinarily passionate about your work and truly love it in order to make things happen.
3. Be really clear on what you want for your business—then fake it till you make it.

What is your personal or professional motto?

If it ain't broke, don't fix it.

What's the first thing you do every morning to start your day on the right foot?

Family hugs.

What's your favorite thing to come home to after a long day of work?

My daughter running toward me with sticky Popsicle hands and face, screaming, "Maaaammmaaaa!!!"

Name the biggest overall lesson you've learned in running a business.

Don't sweat the small stuff. Don't make decisions based on fear. Know when to say no. Have faith in oneself and in the business. Be nice to people. Stay humble. Give back.

> "I tend to take myself and the work apart a lot in the process before finally figuring it out."

Maya Lin

Artist, Architect,
Sculptor, Designer
New York, NY

What was the best piece of business advice you were given when you were starting out?

In architecture school, I was spending as much time making art. Frank Gehry told me not to worry about choosing one or the other and to just continue pursuing both.

Name a fear or professional challenge that keeps you up at night.

Making works that aren't strong.

Name the biggest overall lesson you've learned in running a business.

I don't see my studio as a business—I keep it small and take an art studio approach.

In moments of self-doubt or adversity, how do you build yourself back up?

My process in creativity has always been about doubt and worrying about the project, then exploration, then finding and making the work—I tend to take myself and the work apart a lot in the process before finally figuring it out.

What tool, object, or ritual could you not live without in your workday?

Tea and music and light.

> "Your success and failure are completely in your hands, with every minute decision."

Issa Rae

Writer, Director, Actor
Los Angeles, CA

What did you want to be when you were a child?
I wanted to be a writer, and a dinosaur, and a police officer (briefly).

What characteristic do you most admire in other creative women?
Discipline. It's one thing to write every day—that's already hard enough. But to *complete* something that you're proud of, consistently, is a hard thing to do. I've started *so* many writing projects that I will never finish, just because I get discouraged or lazy or bored. I admire other creative women who say, "I'm going to finish no matter how horrible this piece of shit is."

What does success mean to you?
Being comfortable and happy creating what I love on a consistent basis.

What is your favorite thing about your workspace?
That it's ever-changing. I rotate between my home desk, Starbucks, a coffee shop/restaurant down the street from my house, a café downtown, and the library in my building. I need variation or to feel like I'm stepping into somewhere where others are being productive. It feels like community work that way.

Has learning from a mistake ever led you to success?
I've had several moments where I completely put faith in someone else's instincts (because I thought they were more knowledgeable) and set aside my own. When I stopped doing that, I started to educate myself and became more confident in my creative business decisions.

Name a fear or professional challenge that keeps you up at night.
Being labeled as a bad writer.

In moments of self-doubt or adversity, how do you build yourself back up?
I remind myself that I'm doing what I love and that I'm building up others whom I love too.

What quotation or saying inspires and motivates you to be yourself and do what you love?

Our family mantra: "Give to your world the best, and the best will come back to you."

Which of your traits are you most proud of?
My empathy.

What's the hardest thing about being your own boss that isn't obvious?
That your success and failure are completely in your hands, with every minute decision.

What tool, object, or ritual could you not live without in your workday?
I have to check what's happening in the world (news and gossip) before putting my phone aside and focusing. Otherwise, I have FOMO.

> ## "Treat others as you would want to be treated."

Amada Cruz

Museum Director
Phoenix, AZ

What did you want to be when you were a child?
A ballerina.

What characteristic do you most admire in other creative women?
Fearlessness. It takes courage to stick to your own vision.

If you were given $100 million, would you run your business any differently?
I would endow free admission at the museum.

What is the biggest sacrifice you've made in your career/line of work?
I don't consider it a sacrifice to work in the arts, but rather a privilege. The one thing I do wish I had is more time to just think.

In moments of self-doubt or adversity, how do you build yourself back up?
A healthy amount of professional distance helps you see adversity as a temporary state. It helps to step back from the problem, analyze it, and move on.

What is your personal or professional motto?
Treat others as you would want to be treated.

What does the world need more of? Less of?
Tolerance. Greed.

> "When you start your own business, it's an enormous amount of work and worry. But I don't know if I would call that sacrifice. Buy the ticket, take the ride."

Liz Lambert

Hotelier
Austin, TX

What did you want to be when you were a child?

The first thing I can remember wanting to be, besides a cowboy, was a lawyer. I remember the moment, in second grade, but I don't know where the impulse came from.

What was the best piece of business advice you were given when you were starting out?

I had no idea what I was doing in the beginning, so I sought out a lot of advice. I cold-called Chip Conley (Chip founded Joie de Vivre Hotels and is now the VP of Global Hospitality for Airbnb) because I had read about him in a hotel trade magazine, and asked if he would look at my business plan, which was really just a stack of papers full of wide-eyed conjecture. When he met with me, which was miraculous in and of itself, I had no way to grasp any of the words or concepts that he was using to review my financial assumptions. I had been throwing hopeful darts at a board. Learning to read financial statements and understand cash flow is the only way to keep the doors of a young business open, and it was the most important thing I learned. No matter how creative you are, your thing won't work if you don't understand what makes a business work—and a business is what you want to start.

What's the biggest sacrifice you've made in starting or running your business?

I had a lot of sleepless nights, wondering if I could keep the ship afloat. When you start your own business, it's an enormous amount of work and worry. But I don't know if I would call that sacrifice. Buy the ticket, take the ride.

What does success mean to you?

For me, success is doing what I get to do. To travel, to meet and work with the most interesting people, to be curious about what people manufacture with their minds and hands, and to make a livelihood out of good design and being a good host.

Name the biggest overall lesson you've learned in running a business.

It's been said before, but people are your biggest asset. There is no way that you can be everywhere at once, and you wouldn't want to be. Put the right people in the right place and your job becomes easier. And you have so much to learn from them, thank God. It takes a village.

Has learning from a mistake ever led you to success?

They say in the hospitality industry that more people will remember you for righting a mistake than for having a seamless experience from beginning to end. Mistakes will be made. If you can recover from those mistakes, treat people like you hope they would treat you, then everybody wins.

In moments of self-doubt or adversity, how do you build yourself back up?

There have been tough times all along. I think you just slog through and remind yourself of the vision and the passion and why you are doing what you do in the first place. You read and study. So many people have gone before us, with so much adversity. Brave the storm.

What quotation or saying inspires and motivates you to be yourself and do what you love?

"Some people will tell you that slow is good, but I'm here to tell you that fast is better. I've always believed this, in spite of the trouble it's caused me. Being shot out of a cannon will always be better than being squeezed out of a tube. That is why God made fast motorcycles, Bubba."
—Hunter S. Thompson

At what point in your life did you first learn about your field of work? What called you to it?

I remember going to a hotel in downtown Odessa with my grandfather. He was a rancher, so he didn't have a proper office, and he would take his meetings in the best hotel downtown. A place that offered shoeshines and the Sunday paper. I was tiny—four or five—and he loved having me with him. There were leather couches, and cigar smoke, and men talking business, and deals were sealed with a handshake. My mother loved hotels too. We would go to big cities, and there was an entire ritual around the hotel. I think they both instilled the love of hotels in me.

What is your personal or professional motto?

"Make hay while the sun shines," something my grandmother told me.

Where were you when you came up with the idea for your business or discovered what you wanted to do?

I remember exactly. I was a lawyer, a trial lawyer, in Texas. A good friend of mine, Tony Winik, was dying of AIDS. My brother had been recently diagnosed with HIV, which was a death sentence at the time. He was my North Star. I was taking a shower in a hotel room in San Francisco, and I thought, I have to do what matters for me in life—it's not worth playing it safe, I have to take a risk, no matter what the consequence. I had no idea what I was doing, but I got out of that shower and I was resolved. I went back to Austin and knocked on the door of the San Jose Motel, which I had been staring at out of the window from a barstool for months.

**What is your no-fail go-to when you need
inspiration or to get out of a creative rut?**

Travel. Even if it's just down the block. Or farther. Always go farther. Change your environment, take a trip, go see what other people are doing.

"I admire authenticity and conviction."

Martine Rose

Fashion Designer
London, England

What did you want to be when you were a child?

I loved dancing and performing when I was a child and distinctly remember demanding my family watch me dance. But I actually became shyer and more self-conscious as I got older. Fashion didn't manifest as anything distinct until much later.

What characteristic do you most admire in other creative women?

Authenticity and conviction.

What does success mean to you?

That's hard to define, as it's difficult to quantify success. But if I think about those times when I feel I have communicated successfully, it is somehow gauged with the respect of my peers, in particular with people/designers I respect and look up to. I also teach and can see my work influence a younger generation. Of course, success in my line of work is when I have been able to get the balance right between a fantastic idea and its commercial success.

What is your favorite thing about your workspace?

The big blank wall at the start of each season.

In moments of self-doubt or adversity, how do you build yourself back up?

There isn't one thing that I do; I think it's a collection of things that gets me through. I practice meditation and have been doing that for around ten years. I should do it every day, but during times when I am really struggling, I practice every day and it's an enormous source of comfort and motivation. Also, I rely heavily on my friends and family. I retreat into a space where I can access a sense of scale and perspective, as that is often what I struggle with during those difficult times.

What is your personal or professional motto?

You can't please all the people all the time (professional).

What's the hardest thing about being your own boss that isn't obvious?

Keeping a calm exterior in front of your team when things feel like they are going tits up.

What is your no-fail go-to when you need inspiration or to get out of a creative rut?

The library.

What does the world need more of? Less of?

More freethinkers, fewer corporations.

"Avoid overthinking and allow yourself to be wrong."

Fay Andrada

Jewelry Designer
Brooklyn, NY

What did you want to be when you were a child?

I wanted to be a fashion designer. I'm sure a lot of young girls did at that time. It was peak '80s: Punky Brewster, Madonna, and Denise Huxtable were a major influence on me. Looking back, I'm glad to have had the encouragement to be different. It really stuck with me.

What was the best piece of business advice you were given when you were starting out?

"Just because you don't like it, doesn't mean someone won't like it." A jewelry teacher said this about a piece I was most likely cringing over. I go back and forth about this advice. Is it cynical or mature? On one hand, I would like to think I've never put forth a piece of jewelry I wouldn't wear myself. On the other hand, some weaker designs, over time, have grown on me and become the strongest. I think the important thing is to avoid overthinking and allow yourself to be wrong.

What is your favorite thing about your workspace?

I owe everything to my workspace. I am very lucky that it is nestled within a community of small creative businesses, mostly run by women my age. We have separate studios, but we share the beautiful outdoor areas and often ideas,

meals, and resources. When I moved in, jewelry was more of a hobby than a business. The talent, wisdom, and energy that surround me have pushed me to grow and been a source of support throughout the process.

What is the biggest sacrifice you've made in starting or running your business?

An unexpected sacrifice has been losing a version of myself that I quite liked: the employee. Working within a team to please a boss had its advantages. I got to design all day. I am much less effective running things by myself and often do more admin than design. There is always so much to learn and no one to enforce deadlines or thank you at the end of the day. But eventually, success, in the bigger picture, replaced all those things.

What does success mean to you?

Success has always been a moving target for me. I guess that is human nature. Sometimes, in a surprise respite, I can see how far I've come and force myself to feel successful for a minute. With more age and experience I hope those moments last longer and come more naturally.

Name the biggest overall lesson you've learned in running a business.

To not take things personally. With creative work, it is especially hard to extract your feelings and operate on a purely business level. It is an enormous relief once you do, though. I find that if you feel offended by someone, it's helpful to imagine their boss yelling at them. For example, at my first trade show, I was so disappointed every time someone overlooked my booth. It still stings a bit, but I started imagining the buyer's day from a business perspective. There is a set amount of hours, set amount of designers, and set budget. How can visiting my booth make their job easier?

Has learning from a mistake ever led you to success?

In the beginning, I didn't think to hire people who knew more than I did. I thought being a leader meant knowing the most. This all changed when I was pregnant with my son. I was forced to delegate everything and found that there was no end to what I could learn from the people helping me. It has become essential for me to step back and see what other skills and talents colleagues and coworkers bring to the table.

In moments of self-doubt or adversity, how do you build yourself back up?

I meet with someone, in person, who supports my business. Getting out of the studio, getting out of my head, and seeing the busy city at work, in motion, is a surefire source of both encouragement and inspiration.

In your opinion, what are the top three things someone should consider before starting a business?

Before anyone starts a creative business, I urge them to consider how much administration is required each day. That saying "Find something you love and you'll never have to work again" is a bit false. If you find something you love, you will have to work on selling it, shipping it, and following up on e-mails to get paid for it. I also encourage people to imagine their business through the different stages of their life. What if you move to another state or have a child? And finally, are they prepared for success?

What does the world need more of?

The world needs more people who help creative people start small businesses. There are so many creative people bursting with ideas but with no financial or legal support to start their business properly.

What is your no-fail go-to when you need inspiration or to get out of a creative rut?

I am willing to bet that riding the New York City subway can deliver inspiration to almost anyone in any field.

What's your favorite thing to come home to after a long day of work?

My husband, son, dog, and refrigerator.

"Allow time and life to develop. Things don't happen overnight."

Frances Palmer

Potter
Weston, CT

What was the best piece of business advice you were given when you were starting out?

In the beginning, as a potter making functional work, I struggled to know how to price the pieces. I wanted to be compensated for the great amount of time it took to produce the pot but was concerned about what people would be willing to pay for something that they used, as opposed to "sculpture." My dear friend who is a fine jeweler said that after adding in costs, you have to come up with a price that feels good in your heart. I have followed that advice ever since.

What does success mean to you?

Success means that I can make pots I believe in and that people can enjoy in their environments. I send work around the world. It makes me incredibly happy to think that my customers use my pottery every day and that perhaps it makes their lives a bit more beautiful.

Has learning from a mistake ever led you to success?

Ceramics is trial and error, and every firing is an experiment of sorts. Mistakes are an essential part of the process. This starts with the throwing—the clay often takes you into a form that you had not planned. The firing, the glazing, these are elements that are somewhat out of your control. But, at the end of the day, this is what I find most appealing about the art form. I like being only a part of the result and leaving a bit up to chance as well.

What quotation or saying inspires and motivates you to be yourself and do what you love?

"Rome was not built in a day." That seems to cover just about every aspect of what I do. Meaning, allow time and life to develop. Things such as relationships, work, and goals don't happen overnight.

At what point in your life did you first learn about your field of work? What called you to it?

I have an undergraduate and graduate degree in art history and was familiar with ceramics and civilization. I have always made work with my hands and had a garden. When we moved out to Connecticut full-time with our infant daughter, I wanted to make pots myself to unify the garden, cooking, and making work with my hands.

Which of your traits are you most proud of?

Perseverance.

What is your personal or professional motto?

"A row is a row is a row." This is an adaptation of Gertrude Stein's "A rose is a rose is a rose." I used to knit all the time. If I picked up the needle and knit a row, then I would be that much closer to completion. I use this as a metaphor for accomplishing tasks of every description. People often look for great swathes of time; however, I think things get finished beautifully in steps, especially in ceramics and gardening.

Name a woman (or women), past or present, whom you admire or look up to.

I admire artists like Louise Bourgeois or Lucie Rie. But the women I most admire are my friends, people whom I really know. I have respect for the things they do and the efforts they make on a daily basis. And I am grateful for their friendship.

"In that slowing-down, I find the space where writing happens."

Carolina Ebeid

Poet, Editor
Denver, CO

What did you want to be when you were a child?
According to my father, I once said that I wanted to be a neighborhood ice cream vendor with a truck called "Ice Cream Lady." I recall always wanting to be a writer.

What was the best piece of business advice you were given when you were starting out?
One piece of advice that rings true and that I would pass on to other writers: Read, read, read widely and every day; that's the generative source for all of one's subsequent work. It's important here to acknowledge that the habit of reading may be difficult for many to enter (even for authors) because it requires one to slow down. But in that slowing-down, I find the space where writing happens.

What is your favorite thing about your workspace?
I have been moving a lot in recent years, but in all the houses where I've lived I've been lucky to have a window in my writing space. A window—the natural light that comes through—has always been my favorite.

What does success mean to you?
A poet at her desk writing the next piece.

Name a fear or professional challenge that keeps you up at night.
One does not make much money from poetry; therefore, a poet teaches, or finds a job that will allow time to write. I perpetually fear under-employment or being in a job that affords little time and concentration to write.

Name the biggest overall lesson you've learned in running a business.
I've come to see the wisdom of working on my writing every day. This isn't easy. My natural inclination is to not write. But I can admit now that the act of "writing every day" encompasses so much that seems like inactivity, such as idle-ness and thinking; it encompasses reading and engaging with other art forms. I jot down words on my way to catch a bus, or I'll stop a conversation to record a thought. I carry a notebook, or make use of the Notes app on my iPhone. I'll write down phrases, bits of overheard speech, images, anything worthy of a poem or essay. I'll collect these in a magpie style for later assembling.

Has learning from a mistake ever led you to success?
I am what is called a late bloomer. My first full-length book will be out in 2016. I meet people who expect me to have four books in the world already, perhaps because I am almost forty years of age. I am not prolific, and I work at a slow pace. The mistake I've made is doubting my pacing, and the work itself, though with maturity I have been able to quell those doubts so as to move forward.

In moments of self-doubt or adversity, how do you build yourself back up?
Perhaps I am first answering the reverse of this question. When something good happens in my writing life—say I win a fellowship or award—not too much time passes before little doubts begin feasting on my happiness, and my sense of self or accomplishment turns up dusty, moth-eaten. They made an error, the voices will say, or They gave such-and-such award to your work only because you're Latina. Those kinds of doubts. My poet husband has encouraged me to say *yes* to *yes*.

> "All mistakes teach us something, so there are, in reality, no mistakes. Just things we learn."

Nikki Giovanni

Poet, Professor
Blacksburg, VA

What did you want to be when you were a child?
I hate to answer like this, but I don't think I made any plans when I was little. I liked to read and I always wanted to travel. I am a space geek, so I always thought going into space would be wonderful.

What characteristic do you most admire in other creative women?
Quietness. I admire those who can sit and watch.

What does success mean to you?
Completing the project. Since I am my first reader, I have to be content that I have done my best.

What is your favorite thing about your workspace?
The photographs. I collect antiques, but I also have family photos. I write in a small space because I like small spaces. I like the tucked-in feeling.

If you were given $100 million, would you run your business any differently? How so?
That's quite a bit of money. And since I am a writer, not a product, I would probably enjoy the travel—I've never been to the Australian Open, and I'd like to go to Sweden. I suppose I could buy caviar, but I don't eat caviar anymore because I finally realized the eggs belonged to a female like me. And I am not in any particular need so I'd probably find reasons to be of financial help to folk if I could be.

Has learning from a mistake ever led you to success?
Mistakes are a fact of life; they are building blocks, stepping-stones, the way we learn new things. Columbus wasn't looking for a New World, he was searching for a route to spices. All mistakes teach us something, so there are, in reality, no mistakes. Just things we learn.

In moments of self-doubt or adversity, how do you build yourself back up?
I so seldom doubt myself. If I have questions, I seek answers; if I don't find answers, I keep my computer off and my mouth closed.

Which of your traits are you most proud of?
I am persistent. I will complete the job. I push on.

What's the hardest thing about being your own boss that isn't obvious?
I really love being my own boss because I can run things the way I want. I have three indispensable folks who help me and upon whom I totally depend for their expertise.

Where were you when you came up with the idea for your business or discovered what you wanted to do?
I am a writer and more, a Southerner. We all tell stories. I love reading and talking. I think I started knowing I have a talent when a teacher, Miss Delaney, passed around a paper of mine to other teachers and they commented positively on it.

What does the world need more of?
The world needs more patience, but honesty could help a bit too.

> "Women are the eyes and ears of the universe."

Lizzo

Musician
Minneapolis, MN

What did you want to be when you were a child?
I wanted to be an astronomer. The word on the street (aka my mom) says my first word was *star*.

What is your favorite thing about your workspace?
My workspace doesn't have an opinion. It's comfortable and loves to listen.

What does success mean to you?
Look at the people around you—your family, colleagues, and friends. If they're eating, safe, and happy, then I believe you're successful.

What characteristic do you most admire in other creative women?

The female perspective, in general, is to be admired. We are the eyes and ears of the universe.

What is the biggest sacrifice you've made in your career/line of work?
Love.

Name a fear or professional challenge that keeps you up at night.
I struggle with maintaining authenticity in an industry that thrives on the commerce of art.

In moments of self-doubt or adversity, how do you build yourself back up?
I remember that it doesn't exist.

Which of your traits are you most proud of?
My "spirit of discernment." We all go off vibes, but I can decide if I'm going to vibe with someone within the first ten seconds of meeting a person.

What tool, object, or ritual could you not live without in your workday?
My laptop. She's the air that I breathe.

If you were magically given three more hours per day, what would you do with them?
Exactly what Beyoncé does with them.

What quotation or saying inspires and motivates you to be yourself and do what you love?

"Big GRRRL Small World."

"The world needs more consciousness, less greed."

Shanan Campanaro

Textile Designer
Brooklyn, NY

What did you want to be when you were a child?

I wanted to be an artist, fashion designer, or interior designer.

What was the best piece of business advice you were given when you were starting out? (Or a piece of advice you're glad you ignored?)

I was encouraged to take every possible opportunity. It was when I stopped taking that advice and gave energy only to the right opportunities that things really started to take off for me. Trying to entertain every possible opportunity can really waste a lot of time and energy.

Name a fear or professional challenge that keeps you up at night.

Managing growth and the idea of losing my current team or having to grow the team and not finding the right people are things that I worry about.

Name the biggest overall lesson you've learned in running a business.

I have really learned how to deal with anything in a calm and nonreactionary way. There are so many decisions I have to make and so many unforeseen obstacles or problems or opportunities that end up crossing your path when you are running a business. I have learned that it's really important to take care of yourself and be in tune with who you are and what you want and stand for, so that decision-making can come quicker and second-guessing isn't a problem.

At what point in your life did you first learn about your field of work? What called you to it?

Design just seemed like such a better place for my art than the art world. I had an art degree, but making a painting for one person to have in their house on the wall seemed frivolous. It felt more magnanimous to make things that are reproducible and can be enjoyed by more than one person.

Name your greatest success (or something you're most proud of) in your business experiences.

I am really proud that we can associate what we do with a cause and have introduced our love and care for the environment into our brand messages and our products and materials.

What does the world need more of? Less of?

More consciousness, less greed.

Which of your traits are you most proud of?

Being able to change and get better.

What tool, object, or ritual could you not live without in your workday?

Yoga, meditation, light, tidiness, my pen and tablet.

Name a woman (or women), past or present, whom you admire or look up to.

Georgia O'Keeffe. I love how she lived on her own out in the desert. I love that she ate the same breakfast every day and had her own chef. I love that she lived to almost one hundred years old doing the same thing each day out in nature, and I love her wrinkles and her natural style. Her home and her uniqueness. I admire how she lived more than how she worked. She was so true to exactly how she wanted to live and be.

"We've got to reverse our throwaway culture."

Rebecca Wood

Potter
Athens, GA

What did you want to be when you were a child?

First, an archaeologist. I wanted to discover a new pyramid! Then a weather girl, then a fashion designer, then I just started being an artist!

What was the best piece of business advice you were given when you were starting out?

Before I got into ceramics, I was making hats and scarves for Barneys. I made some bed-size throws, and I laid one out and took a picture of it straight on. Soon after, I visited my sister in New York and met her friend Bob Bauman at a party. He turned out to be the head shoe buyer at Saks for thirty years, so he knew a thing or two. I showed him my picture of the throw, and he said, "Never just show the product. Always show the lifestyle." I got it, and I've been doing it ever since.

What is your favorite thing about your workspace?

The people! My ceramic workspace is r.wood studio, where I go mostly every day. You can't find more intelligent, creative, funny, sweet, and helpful people anywhere. We all have such a good time hanging out and working together to get that r.wood order out the door! It's a wonderful, nurturing, supportive community.

If you were given $100 million, would you run your business any differently? How so?

I think we'd still run it the same, but I can tell you right now we'd insulate and put in heat and air-conditioning. And hire a full-time gardener and chef to grow food and flowers and fix our lunch. Plus, I'd buy everyone a place in the country!

Name the biggest overall lesson you've learned in running a business.

Always be honest with the customer and make them happy.

Has learning from a mistake ever led you to success?

In the beginning, I sold to very few stores, but some were high-profile clients. They always said they would pay net sixty days, but it was more like six months, or never. I had had bad experiences with a couple of big-name stores already. Even though they owed less than $2,000, it was ruining my finances trying to hang on. I was so strung out financially from it all that when Neiman Marcus called and wanted to place a $30,000 order, I basically told them "No way!" The buyer, Bill Mackin, asked me to figure out how much money I would need to fulfill that size order in two months. Just to see, I totaled up all the materials, workers, and equipment I'd have to acquire before I could do it, and it was $19,000. I called Bill Mackin and said it would take $19,000, and he said, "What if I front you the $19,000?" I was still somewhat skeptical, but I told him I'd do it. Sure enough, the check came in the mail and we got started. Having that advance allowed us to instantly boost our production with more kilns, workers, and supplies. From then on, we *could* do a $30,000 order, so our potential was greatly increased, and I'm so thankful for Bill.

In moments of self-doubt or adversity, how do you build yourself back up?

Get in nature.

At what point in your life did you first learn about your field of work? What called you to it?

Even though I was into crafts of all kinds growing up, I was never interested in ceramics. All the pottery I ever saw was at craft fairs, and it was all dark brown or a dull blue-gray. I couldn't figure out why potters were stuck on those dreadful colors. Later in life I learned about colorful glazes, and then I started to get more interested.

Name your greatest success (or something you're most proud of) in your business experiences.

Spawning workers who leave r.wood studio to start their own successful businesses.

In your opinion, what are the top three things someone should consider before starting a business?

After attending trade shows and seeing the amount of stuff soon to end up in landfills—and by that I mean products that are frivolous and not meant to last, or so trendy they'll be over in six months—I think you have to ask yourself, "Is my product just going to end up a burden on mother earth? Is my product recyclable or is it made to last? Is the packaging recyclable?" Look at the carbon footprint. We've got to reverse our throwaway culture.

Name a woman (or women), past or present, whom you admire or look up to.

Björk.

> "In a world where so many are trying to be like the majority, it's refreshing to see women, courageously, own who they are."

Carla Hall

Chef, Television Host
Washington, D.C.

What did you want to be when you were a child?

A Broadway actor. The first play I saw on Broadway was *Bubbling Brown Sugar*, and I was eleven years old. I was intrigued by the actors, the stage, the costumes, the singing. I loved it all, and I wanted to be a part of it.

What characteristic do you most admire in other creative women?

Their ability to be comfortable with their uniqueness, be it their ideas that are out of the box, their fashion sense, their overall quirkiness, or just their confident sense of self. In a world where so many are trying to be like the majority, it's refreshing to see women, courageously, own who they are.

What does success mean to you?

Food has been at the center of my life for over twenty-five years. Years ago I realized that I was making a living, albeit meager, doing exactly

what I loved to do. Success to me is loving something enough to fail at it repeatedly until you get relatively good at it.

What is your favorite thing about your workspace?
When I think about it, I have two workspaces—my kitchen and my dining room table. My dining room table in D.C. is where I do crafts. The dining room is small, but it has three windows that let the morning and afternoon light in. The table is just a big ol' seven-foot wooden table that can hold everything I need.

In moments of self-doubt or adversity, how do you build yourself back up?
I get quiet, and I meditate. I ask myself, "What do I need to learn here?" I know that on the other side of self-doubt or adversity there is victory. The "me" who emerges will be a little stronger and stand a little taller than the "me" who had doubt.

What is the biggest sacrifice you've made in your career/line of work?
Because I work in the food and hospitality world, I'm working when most people are celebrating. I'm also a career changer, so my career didn't really get going until I was in my late thirties, early forties. This was during the time most of my friends were settling down and having families of their own. I, on the other hand, felt like I had some catching up to do in my newly chosen field. I worked seven days a week and fourteen to sixteen hours a day. I missed a lot of family events and I didn't date a lot.

What is your personal or professional motto?

If you're gonna do it, do it with love. I make the decision to have a good attitude about pretty much everything I do.

What's the hardest thing about being your own boss that isn't obvious?
The lack of an employee annual review. There are times when I would welcome a report card from a third party.

What would you tell yourself ten to twenty years ago that you wish you knew then?
Being patient, without judgment, makes you a good employer and employee.

What quotation inspires and motivates you to be yourself and do what you love?
"Courage starts with showing up and letting ourselves be seen." —Brené Brown

Where were you when you came up with the idea for your business or discovered what you wanted to do?
The decision to change my catering company to a cookie company (now cookies and desserts) was the result of deciding to do *Top Chef All-Stars*. I was burned out on catering, and it was suggested that I use the show as part of my business plan. I wasn't sure what that next step was, so in the heat of the moment, I chose petite cookies, which were already a small part of the catering business. The idea of focusing my attention on one thing and doing it well appealed to me.

What's the first thing you do every morning to start your day on the right foot?
I say the following affirmations: God goes before me making things smooth and easy; clearing my way. No person, place, or thing or outside condition can affect me. I am power. I am worthy. I am free. I am creative. I am unique. I am confident. And so it is.

The world needs more face-to-face conversation, perhaps over a meal, so we can really get to know each other without assumptions. The world needs fewer sound bites where those assumptions are formed.

> "I named my company Louise Fili Ltd because I wanted to send a message, which was this: if you have a problem with my being female, then I don't want *you* as a client."

Louise Fili

Graphic Designer
New York, NY

What did you want to be when you were a child?
A novelist. I would write the first chapter, then stop and design the jacket, then move on to the next one.

What was the best piece of business advice you were given when you were starting out?
Get paid up front.

What is your favorite thing about your workspace?
I am very fortunate that my life and work are one and the same. My studio is a walk-in archive of all the restaurant menus, business cards, matchbooks, and specialty food packages I have designed, as well as many posters and flea market finds from decades of traveling in Italy and France. Surrounded by objects that I treasure, I always feel at home, and in this environment I am routinely transported to Europe. This is a workplace where I feel just as comfortable cooking lunch for staff or clients as I do designing.

Has learning from a mistake ever led you to success?
A junior designer once made a $10,000 printing error on a job simply by not taking the time to ask me one question. Fortunately, the printer didn't make me pay, but instead invited me to design a promotion for him, which became one of my favorite pieces.

At what point in your life did you first learn about your field of work? What called you to it?
Even before I knew what graphic design was, I knew it was something that I wanted to do. When I was growing up, this term was hardly in use; it was known instead as the very unsexy *commercial art*. At age sixteen, I sent away for an Osmiroid pen advertised in the back of *The New Yorker* and taught myself calligraphy; I would soon be running a relatively lucrative business making illuminated manuscripts of Bob Dylan lyrics for classmates. Once I got to college I discovered that everything I was interested in—type, calligraphy, making books—was in fact graphic design.

Name your greatest success (or something you're most proud of) in your business experiences.
When I was working on my monograph, I made a vow to myself that when the book was finished, I would take a month off and go to the American Academy in Rome to work on a personal project. I had been photographing shop and restaurant signs all over Italy for over three decades, while watching many of the most beautiful specimens disappear, so I felt a sense of urgency to put them into a book, and therefore return to rephotograph as many as possible before it was too late. After that month, I returned three more times to Italy in that same year in order to finish the book. Even though this was not a smart move in terms of my business, it was well worth it. This project gave me the most pleasure of anything I have ever worked on.

Which of your traits are you most proud of?
When I started my business, it was the pre-Google era, which meant that when you named your

company, you couldn't get too creative. After all, people had to find you. I knew I had to name it after myself, which could have been a liability. I suppose that I could have come up with something like "Fili Associates" to look bigger and more important. In the end I chose Louise Fili Ltd because I really wanted to send a message, which was this: if you have a problem with my being female, then I don't want *you* as a client.

Where were you when you came up with the idea for your business or discovered what you wanted to do?

When my son was born, I took a standard three-month maternity leave, with every intention of returning to my job as an art director at a publishing house. On my first day back, I looked around and thought, I don't want to be here. The next day I started my business.

What is your no-fail go-to when you need inspiration or to get out of a creative rut?

That's easy. I take a trip to Italy.

What tool, object, or ritual could you not live without in your workday?

I have two gelato clients, and part of our arrangement is that there is always gelato and sorbetto at the studio. It never fails to keep staff and clients happy.

What's the first thing you do every morning to start your day on the right foot?

Walk to work. It helps clear my head.

"Creative women see opportunity in everything. They push boundaries."

Mariam Paré

Artist, Designer, Speaker
Naperville, IL

What did you want to be when you were a child?
I wanted to be an art teacher because I thought
they had the best job ever, and access to an endless amount of art supplies.

What characteristic do you most admire in other creative women?
Optimism. When confronted with a challenge,
the creative women I know have optimism as
their default mind-set; they see the glass as
half full rather than half empty. When faced
with adversity, they learn all they can from it. I
admire that creative women see opportunity in
everything. They push boundaries.

What is your favorite thing about your workspace?
My workspace is cozy and has art supplies
crammed into every nook and cranny. I am surrounded by all the things I need to be creative.
It is very comfortable and functional for me as
a wheelchair user. It is the place where I am
most capable.

In moments of self-doubt or adversity, how do you build yourself back up?

I take care of myself. I try to curtail any negative thinking and stoke up positive thinking. I rely on my internal resources. I remind myself to have faith that everything will work out.

Name a fear or professional challenge that keeps you up at night.

I used to feel a lot of anxiety when asked to talk about myself or my art in public situations.

A particularly cringeworthy situation happened to me a few years ago and still haunts me today. I was being interviewed by Katie Couric, which was an amazing experience, but at the same time, completely intimidating for me. When the interview began, my anxieties took over. I felt like I botched the interview. I rambled too long with some answers and stumbled to answer other, simple questions.

From that experience I ultimately realized there is more to an art career than just creating art. As an artist, being able to network, engage, and efficiently communicate with people about your work with some amount of confidence is just as important as making the artwork itself. So instead of turning down opportunities because of my anxiety, I vowed to work through my fears and shortcomings in this area.

Over the years I gained experience being interviewed and speaking in public. I even got a therapist for a short while. The reward has been that I now feel much more comfortable putting myself out there. Sure, being in the public eye can still be a tiny bit stressful for me, but now I am happy to say the benefits far outweigh any discomfort.

What quotation or saying inspires and motivates you to be yourself and do what you love?

Back when I was a teenager in the early '90s, I used to follow the Grateful Dead. Those were some of the best, most free years of my life. There is a lyric from "When I Paint My Masterpiece" that I used to sing to myself as a positive affirmation years later when I struggled through my spinal cord injury and had to learn how to paint with my mouth. The words still have the power today to remind me where I came from, and where I am going. The lyric goes, "Someday life will be sweet like a rhapsody / When I paint my masterpiece." It's a great song. Look it up right now and listen to it. You won't be sorry.

What would you tell yourself ten to twenty years ago that you wish you knew then?

Just under twenty years ago I was newly paralyzed and, at that point, still very discouraged by my new physical limitations. It was hard not to feel defeated by the loss of all the things I used to be able to do. So if I could talk to myself twenty years ago, I would tell myself to focus on my strengths, and not on my weaknesses; on the things I could do and not the things I couldn't do; to strive to excel and hone those skills to the point of excellence. That this was the best strategy to secure my future. I would say to myself that the only real obstacles you have are those you create for yourself.

What's the first thing you do every morning to start your day on the right foot?

It can be easy for me to get off on the wrong track in the morning mentally. I have a few affirmations that I say to myself to get me into the right headspace to face the day with energy, optimism, and courage. I clear my mind of any negative thoughts that I may be reinforcing. And I remind myself of all the things I am grateful for.

Name a woman (or women), past or present, whom you admire or look up to.

Immediately my mind goes to Frida Kahlo. I relate to her art and her life on many levels. In much the same way as Frida, my personal physical disability is fatefully intertwined with my artistic expression. Frida was a pioneer for artists like me. With a truthful and emotional language, she demystified taboos related to disability, pain, and suffering and presented it to mainstream society in a humanizing way. And she was still successful! Her life inspires me deeply.

> "When I was about thirteen, my dad told me 'Everyone is weird,' and that simple statement pretty much changed my life."

Julia Turshen

Cookbook Author
Ulster County, NY

What did you want to be when you were a child?
I have always wanted to create cookbooks.

What characteristic do you most admire in other creative women?
The courage to keep your eyes open and trust your vision, especially your peripheral vision. I've always felt that the best work comes from looking at something in a new way or getting to a familiar place through a new route.

What does success mean to you?
I like using laughter as a unit of measurement. If I'm not enjoying what I'm doing, then I'm not enjoying my day-to-day life, and what's the point of that?

What is your favorite thing about your workspace?
Being surrounded by books that mean so much to me, and having space for my pets to come curl up if they feel like it.

What is the biggest sacrifice you've made in your career/line of work?
By choosing a freelance life, I've given up having someone else pay for my health insurance and the security of a regular paycheck. For me, the benefits of working the way I do far outweigh these sacrifices.

Name a fear or professional challenge that keeps you up at night.
After this book, will there be another?

In moments of self-doubt or adversity, how do you build yourself back up?
Putting my issues or fears in perspective usually helps a lot. I feel like I say the phrase, "Let this be my biggest problem" all the time. At the end of the day, I'm creating cookbooks, I'm not saving lives.

What quotation or saying inspires and motivates you to be yourself and do what you love?
When I was about thirteen, my dad told me, "Everyone is weird," and that simple statement pretty much changed my life. I think of it often. It makes me feel relaxed to be myself and do things my own way and be open-minded about everyone else doing the same.

Which of your traits are you most proud of?
I am addicted to silver linings.

What is your personal or professional motto?
It's just dinner.

What does the world need more of? Less of?
More access to good-quality food and water for everyone. Less overthinking.

What's your favorite thing to come home to after a long day of work?
Cooking dinner just for the sake of cooking dinner and not recording it or measuring a thing.

> "I've learned that the word 'no' has many meanings and is not necessarily a negative thing."

Miko Branch

Beauty Entrepreneur
New York, NY

What did you want to be when you were a child?

When I was a little girl, I wanted to be a beautician, and I always wanted to own a hair salon. It had to be pink!

What was the best piece of business advice you were given when you were starting out? (Or a piece of advice you're glad you ignored?)

The best business advice I ever got was from my grandmother Miss Jessie. She would tell my sister and me to "always use common sense." The business advice I'm grateful I ignored was "You can't do that!"

What is your favorite thing about your workspace?

That it is just so pretty. It is the finished product of what my sister, Titi, and I created together; a comfortable space with a feminine, sophisticated aesthetic, designed to resemble a Parisian hotel. Miss Jessie's Salon is a beautiful, unique oasis for our curly-haired customers to come to and get pampered. Titi and I wanted to create a space in which clients could experience relaxation, in a place exuding chic refinement.

Name the biggest overall lesson you've learned in running a business.

I've learned that the word "no" has many meanings and is not necessarily a negative thing. Sometimes no is a positive thing, and sometimes it's okay to say no.

In moments of self-doubt or adversity, how do you build yourself back up?

I do a self-checklist, asking myself a few key questions:

"Have I been fair?"
"Have I been kind?"
"Did I put in the work?"

If the answer to those questions is yes, then that gives me the confidence to stay the course with whatever I was doing, and to keep moving forward, confident in the decisions I have made.

Name your greatest success (or something you're most proud of) in your business experiences.

That I was able to build something out of nothing. I built my business without any financial support, and through the evolution of my business I was able to not only achieve my professional goals, but also to help so many women with their hair and self-esteem.

Which of your traits are you most proud of?

I've learned to embrace my shortcomings and objectively analyze any of my personal or professional deficits. I've learned not to be fearful of the truth, because I've found that if I really look at and acknowledge what I am less than perfect at, it provides me with the opportunity to make substantial improvements.

Name a woman (or women), past or present, whom you admire or look up to.

I look up to my grandmother Miss Jessie Mae Branch, because she was so independent, so resourceful, so beautiful. She was so dignified, and she did not need a lot of money to possess and exude those qualities.

"Write a mission statement that will endure over time, and stick to it."

Hopie and Lily Stockman

Textile Designers
Los Angeles, CA

What did you want to be when you were a child?
Lily: Georgia O'Keeffe. Or a horse—I wanted to grow up to be a palomino. I am living that dream thanks to my hair care professional.
Hopie: An Olympic figure skater. Peggy Fleming was my perpetual Halloween costume, the subject of a third-grade biography report, and a role model.

What was the best piece of business advice you were given when you were starting out?
H: Write a mission statement that will endure over time, and stick to it. Sage advice from my strategy professor at Harvard Business School.

What is your favorite thing about your workspace?
L: Our studio is on the sixth floor of a 1914 Beaux Arts building smack in the middle of historic downtown L.A., right above the Last Bookstore (our favorite in the city). You can feel the energy young designers, businesses, and restaurants are bringing to an area that until recently was blighted by vacant storefronts. There's a collaborative spirit that's surprised us about downtown L.A.; we can't imagine being anywhere else.

Name a fear or professional challenge that keeps you up at night.
H: Despite all the advice we get to raise financing, expand our product lines, and add onto our India operation, we've taken a path of more deliberate, organic growth. Should we be taking bigger risks with our business? I'm haunted by my business school conversations about women being more financially risk-averse than men. Why is that—and does it change the way I want to run my business?

Name the biggest overall lesson you've learned in running a business.
L: Forget about people-pleasing. I've struggled with this for years, and I think a lot of women can relate. Running a business that's so tethered to social media has forced me to stop fretting over disparaging comments on Instagram or mean e-mails. Sometimes it's a healthy gut check. And sometimes it's meaningless trolling and you just have to let it roll off your back.

Has learning from a mistake ever led you to success?
H: Our biggest mistake was being so transparent about the name of our printing workshop in India. We practically shouted "BAGRU!" from the rooftops, and while this has led to much more work for our master printer's business, it's invariably led to Block Shop copycats and put a strain on our production. Even though it's been a headache, it's also been a valuable lesson in protecting one's business.

In the end we've learned not to fear the copycats, and we remain committed to this level of transparency. We believe in connecting customers to the makers of their products. And we've been heartened to see how much both parties truly value that connection (many of our printers are now on Facebook and Instagram). A brand extends so far beyond its products: it consists of a voice, a viewpoint, a sense of design, a life philosophy, the personalities of its

leadership, and of course storytelling. No one can rip off authenticity, and that's been comforting to us as a small business.

Name your greatest success (or something you're most proud of) in your business experiences.

H: Our first meeting with the twenty-six women in our printing community began with our new community manager, Sonia Jain, at the helm. We were surprised that it was the first time this tight-knit community of friends, mothers, sisters, daughters, and aunties had met as an organized group. The subject in question was their health-care needs, toward which we invest 5 percent of our profits. What started as a health needs assessment ended in singing songs and a proposed Block Shop scarf printed exclusively by women. The most important aspect of our meeting turned out to be holding one in the first place.

The meeting provided a moment of mutual understanding and when you're in a healthy relationship with someone, you listen. You do good work for each other. I feel more pride in our relationship with our printers than I do in any other accomplishment at Block Shop.

Name a woman (or women), past or present, whom you admire or look up to.

L: All my heroines are women who articulate the mood of the times through their given medium. Seventies writers Renata Adler, Joan Didion, Susan Sontag. Painter and desert recluse Agnes Martin. Horticulturist, conservationist, and founder of Joshua Tree National Park Minerva Hoyt. They have a clear point of view, a tireless curiosity, and zero regard for trends or popularity.

H: Edith Wharton, a brilliant student of human nature and aesthetic theory.

What does the world need more of? Less of?

L: More original, critical thinking. Less time online. More listening, less talking (trying to take my own advice).

What tool, object, or ritual could you not live without in your workday?

H: The most important ritual in India is chai. Before any meeting, before a day of printing commences, we sit down over chai and talk life, family gossip, politics.

Knowing what you know now, what would you have done differently when you were first starting out?

H: Sync all your systems up front: Shopify, FedEx, ShipStation, QuickBooks, and bank accounts. The engine that keeps a business running is its software systems, and I wish we'd linked them sooner. One of those unglamorous but thank-yourself-later aspects that is essential to a small business.

If you were magically given three more hours per day, what would you do with them?

L: Stockpile them like a nut-hoarding squirrel and tack one extra day onto the day before a big deadline.

H: Illustrate and cowrite a children's book with my boyfriend about a talking dog that is too shy to speak.

"If this were 1615, I'd have been burned at the stake for what I do, so I'm stoked and grateful."

Neko Case

Musician
Burlington, VT

What did you want to be when you were a child?
A combo veterinarian-artist.

What characteristic do you most admire in other creative women?
I admire people who decide it's worth the huge amount of work to *make* a nonnegotiable block of time to create things and express themselves. Growing up through the Reagan years in the United States, we were beat over the head with the idea that arts and music were a pipe dream and a foolish, almost sinful waste of time.

What does success mean to you?
The decades-long, familial relationships I have with my bandmates (the New Pornographers) and coworkers. I'm proud of us.

What is your favorite thing about your workspace?
It's attached to a restaurant! Thinking on a creative problem burns a lot of calories and I need to eat *constantly*. I also love that my dog can come to work with me and we can take a nap together at the studio.

What is the biggest sacrifice you've made in your career/line of work?
No family. I travel too much to meet anyone, have babies, form bonds, etc. I chose it, so I own it. If this were 1615, I'd have been burned at the stake for what I do, so I'm stoked and grateful. I have had to make a big effort in the last year to learn how to say no to opportunities and relax, though. Relaxing is the hardest 'cause I'm a fidgety "doer." It's unhealthy not to have a balance or any recovery time from a strenuous creative excursion. It's a job made of overtime.

Has learning from a mistake ever led you to success?
The thing I'm most grateful to have missed out on was being signed by a major label. I wanted it *so* bad at twenty-six and I thought it was the only way to do things. That's the myth of the entertainment industry, though: "You're *lucky* to be here, to be chosen, and *we* know what's right for you . . . sign the papers." The fact is, I had no idea how it worked at that point, and I would have been lost in the shuffle. Luckily, I had to learn the business from the ground up. I didn't do it alone—I needed lots of help—but that resulted in lasting bonds and true relationships. Having people near who won't be yes-men can be your biggest asset.

In moments of self-doubt or adversity, how do you build yourself back up?
Spending time at home in the dirt. Dirt and nature bring me back.

Which of your traits are you most proud of?
I'm true-blue. A loyal dog.

What does the world need more of? Less of?
More humility, less infighting.

What would you tell yourself ten to twenty years ago that you wish you knew then?
Stop buying dresses; you hate them.

What's the hardest thing about being your own boss that isn't obvious?
It's so terribly lonely.

"Never say no to yourself."

Sibella Court

Interior Designer,
Stylist, Author
Sydney, Australia

What did you want to be when you were a child?

I recently stumbled upon an autobiography I wrote in sixth grade. The teachers asked us to write stories that chronicled our young lives from when we were born. At the end it asked about the future and I said I wanted to live in a big house and have a shop. I don't have a big house, but I do have the shop!

What was the best piece of business advice you were given when you were starting out?

I'm not very good at taking advice. But the best thing I did, knowing from an early age that bookkeeping was not my forte, was hire a bookkeeper and an accountant right away. It created a tight infrastructure and a strong foundation so I could then do what I wanted and needed to do.

What is your favorite thing about your workspace?

I like that it is a working space. It is not always tidy, and it is forever moving and changing.

What is the biggest sacrifice you've made in starting or running your business?

I don't feel like I've made any sacrifices. I wrote my own job description to incorporate all the things I love to do.

Name a fear or professional challenge that keeps you up at night.

I have a fear of idleness. I often think of more skills I should master so I can lend a hand at all times, from carpentry to CAD (computer-aided design), upholstery, painting—you name it, it crosses my mind.

Name the biggest overall lesson you've learned in running a business.

I am continuously learning. Constantly working on and improving communication within a business is so crucial.

At what point in your life did you first learn about your field of work? What called you to it?

I was at university finishing my history degree in 1993. My best friend, Edwina McCann, who at the time was working at *Vogue* (and is now the editor of *Vogue* Australia), thought I might like to assist the former interiors editor at *Vogue Living*. Once I'd arrived in the industry, it was an instantaneous love affair. What I wasn't aware of was that my aunt, who had died of cancer not that long before, was one of the top stylists and editors in Australia. Photographers I worked with knew her and would come up to me with tears in their eyes. She had earned enormous respect in the industry. It is interesting how the world works.

What does the world need more of?

I love the Royal Society of London of the eighteenth century and how they questioned, experimented with, and rethought everything, never just accepted anything as it was. There is no inhibition in invention. Never say no to yourself.

What is your no-fail go-to when you need inspiration or to get out of a creative rut?

A go-to for me is nature, a beachcombing jaunt or a coastal walk. It never fails and always gifts me something incredible, whether it's the colors in the sky or sea, a bird's feather, a sea-tossed pebble, the flotsam and jetsam that has been washed ashore—it is the ultimate in color combination, shape, vista, proportion, layering, tactility. And there's nothing better for getting rid of the cobwebs than a bit of fresh air.

"I was told to do what I loved and not to veer from that."

Maira Kalman

Artist, Author
New York, NY

What did you want to be when you were a child?
I am sure I wanted to be a writer. Solitary, but well-adjusted and good-natured.

What was the best piece of business advice you were given when you were starting out?
I was told to do what I loved and not to veer from that.

What is your favorite thing about your workspace?
The great amount of wall space on which to put up so many images to look at.

Name the biggest overall lesson you've learned in running a business.
Patience and perseverance.

Has learning from a mistake ever led you to success?
I make mistakes every day. But we always say, "Mistakes bring good." Taking on a job that turns out to be a bad fit and quitting the job. You feel a million pounds lighter. Relief prevails.

What's the first thing you do every morning to start your day on the right foot?
Drink a cup of coffee and read the obits.

od Morning Mirali!

I want to go with
to the Central Park this
orning
Be Wake me up!

thank you
Tali

Nº045

Walter
Benjamin

Introduction / Einführung:
Nikola Doll

In moments of self-doubt or adversity, how do you build yourself back up?

I remember that I have deadlines and really have no choice.

What quotation or saying inspires and motivates you to be yourself and do what you love?

"Imagination is more important than knowledge." —Albert Einstein

At what point in your life did you first learn about your field of work? What called you to it?

When I was unhappy with my writing, I began to do cartoons. Saul Steinberg was a great influence. Magazine work seemed delightful.

Which of your traits are you most proud of?

Curiosity. Humor.

Name your greatest success (or something you're most proud of) in your business experiences.

Illustrating *The Elements of Style*. But beyond that, continuing to work and find wonderful projects for over forty years. Though forty years does not sound like so much.

What is your no-fail go-to when you need inspiration or to get out of a creative rut?

Going for a walk.

Name a woman (or women), past or present, whom you admire or look up to.

Eleanor Roosevelt. My mother, Sara Berman.

"Being prolific is necessary to being professionally successful."

Wendy Maruyama

Artist, Designer, Sculptor
San Diego, CA

What did you want to be when you were a child?

As a child, I loved making art, making things with my hands. My mom made me take a summer typing class because it could be a way that I could "make a living." I absolutely sucked at typing. It never dawned on me that being an artist was an option, but I was determined to make it an option after that typing class.

What was the best piece of business advice you were given when you were starting out?

The best thing that I learned was less about business and more about being an artist, and that was to be prolific. I don't believe that everything we make is successful, but to make the one successful piece that does come out, one has to make nine others to get to that point. To that end, I believe that being prolific is necessary to being professionally successful.

What is the biggest sacrifice you've made in starting or running your business?

I don't know if it was a "sacrifice," but I would say my work was a priority. As a result, my social life took the back burner and I didn't really have many relationships. I just got married seven years ago at the age of fifty-five, and I am now convinced that is the perfect age to get married!

Name the biggest overall lesson you've learned in running a business.

To ask for the money first. Not everyone is honest. I am still working on asking for enough money for myself. It's hard.

What quotation or saying inspires and motivates you to be yourself and do what you love?

"You can't use up creativity. The more you use, the more you have." —Maya Angelou

At what point in your life did you first learn about your field of work? What called you to it?

I decided after high school (1970) that I would major in crafts. I took a crafts class in junior college, which I loved, and worked with textiles, ceramics, wood, and metals. The wood assignment mesmerized me because I recall that in high school, we girls were not allowed to take woodshop. Most folks chose to make bowls, pot pipes, cutting boards, etc. I chose to make a three-legged chair with a leather sling seat. It was a revelation for me to discover at that time that working in wood was not men's work after all. And as I took more classes, I realized that making furniture, not woodworking, was a primary interest for me. I was not a tool weenie or into wood grains and cutting joints, but I loved the idea of making furniture as an art form.

Name your greatest success (or something you're most proud of) in your business experiences.

I am proud that I have stuck it out with what I do. It's hard work. There are a lot of ups and downs that come with this territory, but I love it so much that I persevered. I'm also really proud of my students. I have taught for thirty-five years, and while there were some very challenging moments for me as an educator, I feel that my life has become so rich and full with thirty-five years' worth of former students who have stayed in touch and remained friends. I am very proud of their accomplishments and what they have achieved.

"Jump in fearlessly."

Lorna Simpson

Artist, Photographer
Brooklyn, NY

What did you want to be when you were a child?
A ballerina and an artist.

When did you first discover what you wanted to do with your life?
When I was onstage dancing as a child and realized I didn't want to be a dancer. I thought, "Ah . . . now I get the audience thing. I don't like that." I'd rather be watching. I knew I would end up doing something that involved observing behind the scenes.

What was the best piece of advice you were ever given when you were starting out? (Or a piece of advice you're glad you ignored?)
When my daughter was four or five months old, a gallery director said to me, "You know, when women have children it really affects their career negatively." And I said, "*Really*?" and he proceeded to say that I better "gird my loins" for the effect that parenthood would have on my career. I ignored what he said and didn't take it personally and saw it as his own shortcoming, not mine.

What quotation or saying inspires and motivates you to be yourself and do what you love?
"If you're going to try, go all the way. Otherwise, don't even start. This could mean losing girlfriends, wives, relatives, jobs and maybe your mind. It could mean not eating for three or four days. It could mean freezing on a park bench. It could mean mockery, isolation. It's a test of your endurance, of how much you really want to do it. And you'll do it despite the rejection and the worst odds and it will be better than anything you can imagine. If you're going to try that, go all the way. There is no other feeling like that."
—Charles Bukowski

What is your favorite thing about your workspace?
It's perfect; it's amazing. It was designed by David Adjaye. I could not have dreamt of a better space.

If you were given $100 million, would you run your business any differently? How so?
No, I wouldn't run it any differently. I'd run it *quicker*.

Name the biggest overall lesson you've learned in running a business.
To not be afraid of change. To commit to what it takes to do business and be clear about that.

Name your greatest success (or something you're most proud of) in your business experiences.
This past May in Venice, I pulled together a group of paintings for a show. It was my first time showing that sort of work. It was really rewarding that the work was well received.

Which of your traits are you most proud of?
I try to be straightforward and present to hear what other people have to say.

Is there any advice you'd offer to someone looking to start their career?
Jump in fearlessly.

What's the first thing you do every morning to start your day on the right foot?
Close the bedroom door so I make sure the dog doesn't get on my bed.

Name a woman (or women), past or present, whom you admire or look up to.
My mother and both of my grandmothers. They were women who came from other countries or moved from the South to the Midwest for various reasons, and all had very strong personalities.

"Speak less, speak better."

Klancy Miller

Writer, Chef
New York, NY

What did you want to be when you were a child?
When I was little, I wanted to be a lot of things. There was a time when I wanted to be president of the United States of America so I could boss everyone around.

What was the best piece of business advice you were given when you were starting out? (Or a piece of advice you're glad you ignored?)
When my interest in food was developing, before I went to culinary school, a friend's dad said, "You can't make any money in restaurants." I'm glad I pursued my love of food and cooking anyway. I've learned not to be motivated solely by money—it's important, but you should follow your interests, curiosities, and passions without hesitation.

What is the biggest sacrifice you've made in starting or running your business?
The biggest sacrifice I've made has been my social life. I'm driven by due dates, and sometimes I have to hibernate and put my social life on hold to get the work done. My creative process is also often a bit solitary. The French have a saying, though: *Parlons peu, parlons mieux*, which means "Speak less, speak better." I like to think that my catch-ups with friends are even better when we haven't seen each other in a while. The conversations are fuller, juicier.

Has learning from a mistake ever led you to success?
I'm not sure if it's a mistake so much as a notable failure that I learned from. A few years ago, before my first cookbook came to life, I wanted to write a food memoir with recipes about my time in Paris. I was so excited about this project and dove into writing the proposal and actual book with zeal. My agent pitched it to over thirty publishing houses and no one wanted it. She also sent me dozens of their responses. Thankfully, none of them were cruel. I was devastated that my brilliant book idea was not so brilliant in the eyes of others. All told, the whole process was about six months to a year from the writing of the proposal and first chapters to the end of the pitching process. The lesson I learned was to get back up and keep trying and to let go of the disappointment. I also learned that sometimes you work hard and passionately on something you love, and it may not work out. That's okay. You live to tell about it. You come up with other ideas and something will grow. Something will work if you're just patient and persistent.

Name your greatest success (or something you're most proud of) in your business experiences.
The thing I'm most proud of is getting a book deal to write *Cooking Solo*, my cookbook for single people. It was an idea that was right under my nose and came from my own experiences of years of cooking for myself and finding great joy in it. I'm happy to share my philosophy that making a delicious meal for one is a fabulous way to nourish and nurture yourself.

Which of your traits are you most proud of?
The core characteristics I appreciate about myself are enthusiasm, compassion, stamina, patience, persistence, and humor.

What's the first thing you do every morning to start your day on the right foot?
I begin each day by articulating gratitude for waking up. I think all good things come from gratitude—being aware of all the good that already is around you or in you. Sometimes I begin with meditation—not always, though.

> "As long as my work continues to foster joy, celebration, community, generosity, and simplicity, I'm on the road to success."

Dana Tanamachi

Artist, Graphic Designer
Seattle, WA

What did you want to be when you were a child?

My mom always reminds me that I wanted to be either a taxi driver or an elevator operator when I grew up. When I got to elementary school, I wanted to be an architect. I'd spend a lot of time drawing blueprints of my "dream home," which always included a special room for all my hypothetical dogs to play in. I guess I liked the structure and rigidity of designing a home—with all its straight lines and boundaries. But within that framework, I always had a lot of fun. I think that's a pretty accurate depiction of who I am now, actually. Eight-year-old me knew what was up.

What does success mean to you?

To me, success means staying true to the vision and values I held before ever setting out to be "successful." As long as my work continues to foster joy, celebration, community, generosity, and simplicity, I'm on the road to success.

What is your favorite thing about your workspace?

My desk. It's a ten-foot farmhouse table that an interior designer scored for me at a Ralph Lauren floor sample sale in Manhattan. There's so much room to work on it—I can have a big mess of sketches and printouts at one end, and still have my pristine workspace at the other. I also feel like the table is a perfect anchor for the room.

What is the biggest sacrifice you've made in starting or running your business?

When business began picking up extremely fast, I admit that I left a few friends hanging. I definitely made sure to apologize profusely, beg for forgiveness, and realign my values in order to make them a priority. Without healthy relationships, we can become work-obsessed zombies.

Name the biggest overall lesson you've learned in running a business.

Running a business is incredibly difficult at times, but it can be so rewarding. The biggest lesson I've learned is to not invest yourself so heavily in one thing, one trend, or one medium. When I began creating typographic chalk murals in 2009, I never saw chalk as the pinnacle of my career, or the specialty niche I'd always be in. It was a means to an end. And when I felt that season needed to be put to rest, it wasn't devastating at all. It was simply time to walk away. Closing that door opened so many new ones, and I can't imagine where I'd be if I was still clinging on to the thing that had provided so much attention and opportunity. It would only be out of fear. Styles change, tastes change, and people change—especially you!

Has learning from a mistake ever led you to success?

I remember when I got the call from Oprah's set stylist back in 2010 to work on the cover of the February 2011 issue of *O* magazine. I was on the phone with her but was so incredibly stressed out from all the other work I had going on that I wasn't really listening to her at all. In fact, she explained the entire concept to me, but I had somehow missed the fact that it would be the *cover image*, not just an interior illustration. So, I tried to politely turn her down and she basically stopped me in my tracks. She gasped and said, "Did you hear me correctly? I SAID THE COVER OF *O* MAGAZINE. This is not something you turn down!" And she was right. I learned then and there that I should never be so stressed out or so blind so as not to see the giant flashing lights right in front of my face. I knew I needed help! Shortly after that, I began working with a project manager, and it was so nice to get a big chunk of my time (and sanity) back.

What quotation or saying inspires and motivates you to be yourself and do what you love?

"Live a quiet life and work with your hands" has always been my mantra and filter for the things I create. I'm a textbook introvert, and nothing brings me more joy than to sit down at my desk and draw something into being.

Name your greatest success (or something you're most proud of) in your business experiences.

I still pinch myself when I see the cover of *Time* magazine with my work on it!

What does the world need more of? Less of?

The world needs more inspired, original work. It probably needs fewer Pinterest boards full of other people's work.

If you were magically given three more hours per day, what would you do with them?

I love taking continuing education classes. Last year, I took a screen printing course, and most recently I took a ten-week Japanese language class. If I had three more hours per day, I'd definitely take a class—maybe weaving, block printing, or Japanese 2!

> "If I want to do something, I don't let busy stand in the way. I make the time to do it."

Debbie Millman

Writer, Artist, Educator,
Radio Host
New York, NY

What did you want to be when you were a child?

For a while I wanted to be a musician, then an artist, then a journalist. There might have been a time I wanted to be all three at once. As far back as I can remember, I loved to make things. I made my own coloring books, paper dolls, and dioramas, and I even tried to make my own perfume by crushing rose petals into baby oil. I made barrette boxes out of Popsicle sticks, key chains out of lanyards, ashtrays out of clay, and Halloween costumes out of construction paper and old sheets. I even handmade an entire magazine when I was twelve with my best friend. Her name was Debbie also, and we named the magazine *Debutante*. We were very proud of it. I never considered *not* doing something creative with my life.

What is your favorite thing about your workspace?

I love that it is mine! It took a long time for me to get here, and it is something I cherish with every fiber of my being. I also adore the light, and I enjoy that I have so many of the things I

love dearly so close by. I find that magical and amazing and somewhat miraculous.

What quotation or saying inspires and motivates you to be yourself and do what you love?

I was interviewing the great writer Dani Shapiro, and we were talking about the role of confidence in success. She stated that she felt that confidence wasn't as important as courage, and that the action to *do* something was much more critical to success than the idea that you feel confident about doing it. The notion that courage is more important than confidence has stayed with me ever since.

Name the biggest overall lesson you've learned in running a business.

No matter how good you are or how popular you are or how fabulous you are, there are still business cycles. Nothing lasts forever (well, except maybe Styrofoam), and there are always going to be ups and downs, no matter how much you try to avoid the downs.

Knowing what you know now, what would you have done differently when you were first starting out?

I wish I had known that anything worthwhile takes a long time. I wish I had known that things would turn out okay by the time I was in my forties. I wish I had known enough not to be so afraid to go after what I really wanted.

What does the world need more of? Less of?

More patience. Less arrogance.

Which of your traits are you most proud of?

My ability to stay creative and continually make new things. I think kids lose creativity when they feel the only way they can fit in is to conform. Creativity requires a personal belief that you have something meaningful to say or contribute. If this belief gets squashed or hindered, it can fundamentally damage the neurological pathways responsible for creative connections and communication.

If you were magically given three more hours per day, what would you do with them?

I would make things. Lots of things.

Name a fear or professional challenge that keeps you up at night.

Aging and being irrelevant. Having my best work or years behind me.

What is your personal or professional motto?

Busy is a decision. We do the things we want to do, period. If we say we are too busy, it is just shorthand for the thing being "not important enough" or "not a priority." Busy is not a badge. You don't find the time to make things, you make the time to do things. If I want to do something, I don't let busy stand in the way. I make the time to do it.

What is your no-fail go-to when you need inspiration or to get out of a creative rut?

Sleep. Sleep and more sleep.

Name a woman (or women), past or present, whom you admire or look up to.

Gloria Steinem. She paved the way for so many with great intelligence, deep wit, huge empathy, a spectacular sense of humor, and a profound resonance and resilience you rarely see in anyone, man or woman.

What does success mean to you?

I think success is a practice, sort of like love or happiness.

> "I love seeing brilliant, creative women making space and laying down tracks for other women."

Carrie Brownstein

Musician, Writer, Actor
Portland, OR

What did you want to be when you were a child?

A marine biologist or a veterinarian. I also wanted to be an actor or a tennis pro. I always vacillated between wanting to work with animals and wanting to perform for an audience. Perhaps only if I'd become a clown who could shape puppies from balloons could I have achieved both. Writing and performing won out in the end.

What's the first thing you do every morning to start your day on the right foot?

I have always been a morning person, but now I find myself getting up between five and six a.m. every day. I feel like I am stealing daylight hours being awake so early, and even the largest metropolises are quiet at this hour. The stillness helps me to think. The first thing I do is make coffee and read the paper; feeling engaged and part of the world allows me to orient myself, it posits me in the here and now, it wakes me up. Then I head out on a hike or walk. I don't bring my phone, but I bring a small notepad. I jot down ideas. Or I don't. It's like meditation: there are no wrong thoughts, just being. Then I come home and write.

Has learning from a mistake ever led you to success?

When my band Sleater-Kinney went on hiatus, I felt like it was a failure on my part. I had allowed anxiety to become the dominant narrative in my life: it filled up rooms, it dictated interactions and decisions. What came from that very devastating split was a determination to explore and mine my interior landscape, to seek clarity and balance. From there I created *Portlandia* with Fred Armisen, wrote a memoir, and eventually re-formed Sleater-Kinney. Most important, I became a better friend and creative partner.

What characteristic do you most admire in other creative women?

Generosity. I love seeing brilliant, creative women making space and laying down tracks for other women. It's easy to fall into the pernicious trap of thinking that just because you scrapped your way toward achieving your goal, there's no room for anyone else. I also think generosity can apply to both self-care and care of others, allowing yourself time away from work, allowing mistakes, allowing forgiveness. To me generosity is openness, and openness is crucial for creativity.

What does success mean to you?

Knowing someone feels a connection with the work I'm doing. Success also means respect, happiness, friends, and love.

What is your no-fail go-to when you need inspiration or to get out of a creative rut?

I watch films and listen to music until I am bored by my own inertia and inspired by other people's motivation.

In moments of self-doubt or adversity, how do you build yourself back up?

Cry. It's like a reset button.

> "Success is contextual and fleeting, so when things are harmonious, even for a moment, I try to savor it."

Ping Zhu

Illustrator, Artist
Brooklyn, NY

What did you want to be when you were a child?
A ballerina, thanks to *Swan Lake*.

What was the best piece of business advice you were given when you were starting out?
That there is always more to life than work, and to not neglect nurturing a counterbalance even if it seems difficult.

What is your favorite thing about your workspace?
It is shared with other freelancers I admire for different reasons, whether it's their work ethic or their character. It's great to find a group of people who are also interested in maintaining a healthy mix of support and constructive criticism, but who can talk about things aside from work as well.

What does success mean to you?
Success is contextual and fleeting, so when things are harmonious, even for a moment, I try to savor it.

Name the biggest overall lesson you've learned in running a business.
Self-discipline and organization is a must.

Has learning from a mistake ever led you to success?

When I lived in London, my flat was broken into because I had forgotten to double lock the door, and the burglars just kicked it in. My computer was stolen as well as a few other things, but I had been working on my first illustrated book at the time and all my progress was digital. Luckily, I had just backed up the day before so I only lost a day's worth of work. Had I not done that, there would be no book to show for it. The book, *Swan Lake*, was published a few months later and led to a lot of new clients (some of whom are still clients today) and work that related to my childhood love of ballet. But the lesson learned is, always lock your door and always back up your files. *Always.*

In moments of self-doubt or adversity, how do you build yourself back up?

Embrace discomfort and allow for all possibilities for the sake of learning.

What quotation or saying inspires and motivates you to be yourself and do what you love?

"Stay hungry."

What does the world need more of? Less of?

More teachers (who get paid much more than they do now). Fewer flip-flops.

Which of your traits are you most proud of?

Endurance.

Name a woman (or women), past or present, whom you admire or look up to.

My best friend, Christine Wu, who is an incredible fine artist and human. She's influenced and shaped the person I am today, thanks to her nonjudgmental nature and empathy, which has allowed me to become more open-minded and confident with my life choices. I think we also have ESP, which is pretty handy and great.

> "It's important to have people who can relate. Living an artist's life and traveling a bunch—it can be hard to talk about those things with people who don't understand them."

Laura Jane Grace

Musician, Songwriter
Michigan

What did you want to be when you were a child?

I wanted to be in a band. I wanted to be a musician. My first moments of self-recognition were when I first saw Madonna. It was like, "I wanna be that."

What characteristic do you most admire in other creative women?

Drive, ambition, and discipline.

What does success mean to you?

Feeling like you created what you wanted to create and it connected with an audience or with one person in the way you wanted it to.

What is the biggest sacrifice you've made in your career/line of work?

There comes a point when you've gone through a bunch of things in life, where you get over the adolescent view of, "Why is this happening to me?" Where you just realize that that's life and shit happens to everybody. And that being committed to what you're doing means that's just part of it too. You have to take the good and the bad. As a band, we've been hit by semi trucks, gone through lawsuits, had friends die—we've fought; we've all gone through divorces. With the exception of my daughter, there's nothing I would put before what I do, because that's what I need to do to survive.

Has learning from a mistake ever led you to success?

Going through a lawsuit—we were sued by a former manager—was a pretty big thing for me. Looking back on the experience, I needed to get knocked down a little bit, in a way. There was nothing malicious that happened and it all worked out; it was a real exercise in stupidity. Going through that and coming out the other side was really healthy in the end.

Name a fear or professional challenge that keeps you up at night.

I'm obsessive-compulsive—all the fears keep me up at night. Any time you write a song or make a record, there's always that constant question of "Are we ever going to do it again? Or do it as well?" Any time you finish a tour you're like, "Are we ever going to tour again? Is something going to change, is something going to happen?" There's the fear of—is it all worth it? The time you spent away, the people in your past who are no longer in your life whom you have to move on from. I don't sleep well.

How important is it to share your time with people who do what you do or share your background?

It's important to have people who can relate. Living an artist's life and traveling a bunch—it can be hard to talk about those things with people who don't understand them. Having people who understand those things is essential.

What quotation or saying inspires and motivates you to be yourself and do what you love?

Maybe it's a cliché, but the Serenity Prayer. I'm not religious and I didn't grow up in a religious family, but the Serenity Prayer is something my grandmother passed down to me; she had a tapestry with it woven into it.

What does the world need more of? The world needs more understanding overall. Realizing that not everyone has had the same experiences and doesn't have the same perspective, so they're coming from a different place. Trying to recognize that—when you do see a broader picture—you account for more things in it.

What would you tell yourself ten to twenty years ago that you wish you knew then?

Just relax. It will all be okay.

What tool, object, or ritual could you not live without in your workday?

A pen and a piece of paper.

What's your favorite thing to come home to after a long day of work?

A quiet house, a bottle of red wine, and a joint.

Name a woman (or women), past or present, whom you admire or look up to.

My mother.

If you were magically given three more hours per day, what would you do with them?

I'd stay up a lot later.

> "We need less posturing and more honesty about the life of a working artist."

Veronica Corzo-Duchardt

Graphic Designer, Artist
Philadelphia, PA

What did you want to be when you were a child?

I wanted to be an archaeologist. I was a child in the '80s and I was obsessed with movies like *Indiana Jones and the Temple of Doom* and *The Goonies*. I loved the idea of uncovering an ancient site and touching an object that nobody had touched in centuries and that revealed stories of another world. Since I didn't have access to any ancient sites, I would do my digging at my grandparents' house. When I was a kid, my grandfather used to pick me up from school every day. While he was doing something else I would sneak downstairs to his desk, and I'd rummage through his stacks of ledger papers and tax forms, looking for hidden treasure or clues to a possible mystery that I could piece together. I never got very far, since my "digs" came to an abrupt stop once my grandfather found out what I was up to. But my interest in uncovering the hidden histories of objects is something that drives my artistic practice today.

What is your favorite thing about your workspace?

I love being surrounded by the things that influence me. I have a lot of reference materials—personal objects, books and paper ephemera from or about Cuba, office supplies—that I use to create images and textures for my prints. Despite all this, I keep a relatively minimal workspace; I need to have a clear space to think. Most of these materials and objects are stored in boxes that I use much like an archive, pulling them out when I want to engage with them. That's when I play and make a mess of things. When I'm actually working on stuff, I need to spread out and be able to see everything.

What resources would you recommend to someone starting a creative business?

Your best resource is the company you keep. Surround yourself with creative, smart people whose work you respect.

In moments of self-doubt or adversity, how do you build yourself back up?

When I'm doubting myself or having a hard time, I turn to my wife and a few close friends. It's really important to surround yourself with people who are supportive. They usually help me put things into perspective. And at the very least, they'll make me a strong whiskey cocktail and tell me how awesome I am, which doesn't hurt.

What quotation or saying inspires and motivates you to be yourself and do what you love?

"The doing is the thing. The talking and worrying and thinking is not the thing." —Amy Poehler

Has learning from a mistake ever led you to success?

There have been a couple of times in my life where I have relied too much on other people for my own success. I've put my eggs in their basket, hoping they could do something for me that I was too afraid to stand up and do for myself. It came from a place of fear and self-doubt; I let them take the lead, thinking it was something I could never do on my own. Those situations never work out. It took me a while to realize I needed to take responsibility for myself, for my own success and for my own failures. I realized that in order to succeed, I needed to trust myself more, and sometimes that means being more vulnerable. Fear and self-doubt are things I still struggle with at times—we all do—but I've gotten a little better each time at jumping in anyway.

What was the best piece of business advice you were given when you were starting out?

"At the end of the day, it's what you make that matters." I got this advice from a close artist friend of mine as I was starting my studio practice, and it always reminds me to get outside my head and get to work.

Name your greatest success (or something you're most proud of) in your business experiences.

The work I'm proudest of is a project I did called the Neche Collection, named after my grandfather. This was a personal project for me and I wasn't really sure how it would be received. What made it so amazing was that I was able to take all these objects that were so full of specific history for me and translate them into an abstract visual language that was both deeply personal and also allowed people to see their own stories reflected in those abstract images. It brought together my interests in history and personal narrative—which I had engaged in as an artist in grad school—with my abstract, minimal design aesthetic.

Name a woman (or women), past or present, whom you admire or look up to.

Kathleen Hanna [page 342]. I think she's a badass. I admire her as an artist and a musician. But also, as someone who is an introvert, I'm in awe of her fearlessness, the way she is so unapologetically herself and an outspoken feminist. I also love watching her perform—she's mesmerizing. I'm really thankful we have her in the world.

What's the first thing you do every morning to start your day on the right foot?

Every morning my wife and I have coffee in bed together. We talk about what we are doing that day, or listen to NPR, which usually leads us to interesting discussions. I just really like talking to her, and it's so great to do it before the stress of the day falls on us and pulls us in different directions. It's nice that we get to start the day on our own terms, together. If we miss it for whatever reason, I always feel like I'm drifting.

What does the world need more of? Less of?

I think we need more open and honest conversations about success. It's so easy to compare yourself to other people, especially with the Internet giving us peeks into everyone's lives. But it's also easy to forget the parts of their lives that they don't share. The shitty jobs they've had to take to pay rent, the rejections, the depression, the anxiety, the partner who is supporting them with a high-paying job. All the things they tried and failed at before getting to where they are now. We end up comparing ourselves to these perfect, incomplete versions of people that are impossible to measure up to. We need less posturing and more honesty about the life of a working artist.

Name the biggest overall lesson you've learned in running a business.

You can't do it all. You need to choose what's most important to you and go after it. And that can change at different points in your life, so it's important to be flexible and react to the moment. Put your efforts toward the things that are important to you and that you do best, the things that only you can do.

> "Laughter is the ultimate definition of success."

Abbi Jacobson

Writer, Illustrator, Actor, Comedian
Brooklyn, NY

What did you want to be when you were a child?

I think, bizarrely, I wanted to be exactly what I've become. I wanted to be an actor, but that always felt like this impossible dream. An artist was the other half, and as a kid I was always drawing. My brother and I were both art majors in high school and college and both my parents are ridiculously creative, so it was hammered into us from the get-go.

What characteristic do you most admire in other creative women?

I'm really inspired by being curious and going after ideas through all sorts of mediums. Someone like Maira Kalman [page 191]—she has such a specific and beautiful voice that carries over into whatever endeavor she's embarking on. You can tell it's hers—her drawing, her painting, her writing, her compilations of objects—it always seems to stem from an intense curiosity for people and places and things. I try to look at the world in that way.

What is your favorite thing about your workspace?

I like having all my tools around me—all my pens and markers and rulers, etc. I like to decorate with tools so they hopefully inspire me to create more stuff.

B. Smaller

thing didn't work out. She's all
d I'm more 'Broad City.'"

Bad
Bitches
Unite.

What does success mean to you?

I'm realizing that being successful is less about money and more about confidence. I feel most successful when I feel most powerful in who I am and what I want to create and put out into the world. In part of my line of work I also get to have an instant success barometer: laughter. Laughter is the ultimate definition of success for me.

Has learning from a mistake ever led you to success?

I don't know if it was a "mistake," but a big part of the beginnings of the web series *Broad City* was Ilana [Glazer] and me not getting on house teams at the theater where we were training. I'd auditioned three years in a row, and gotten called back, and I just felt so close. I had such tunnel vision, and getting on those teams felt like the whole world and the *only* way I was going to advance my career as a performer. So after three years we were bummed. We decided to make something ourselves. We thought we were geniuses; why were we waiting for other people to "let" us do comedy? So we made *Broad City*. Making that series taught me so much and gave me so much confidence, it's unbelievable. It's the old saying, "When one door closes, another door opens"—except you have to build the other door and pry it open yourself. When you do it that way, you're walking into a place of your own design.

What quotation or saying inspires and motivates you to be yourself and do what you love?

When I was in college, I went to a bookstore and copied down all the quotes off those quotable cards on display into a tiny little book. The one that really stuck with me: "Whatever you can do or dream you can do, begin it. Boldness has genius and power and magic in it. Begin it now."

What would you tell yourself ten to twenty years ago that you wish you knew then?

It's okay to not know exactly what you want to do. All your interests are important and you'll find a way to make them work together—so keep doing everything you enjoy! I tell myself that now.

Which of your traits are you most proud of?

I think I'm pretty versatile. I'm really proud of myself for continuing to do illustration work and incorporating that into my career in new ways. I wish I could do even more.

What's the hardest thing about being your own boss that isn't obvious?

Finding the right people to work with. Even though you might technically be your own boss, you're still going to have to work with a lot of different people. Finding smart, collaborative people whom you work well with is the key to any successful endeavor. I've found so far that it's the people who can be the best but also the hardest part of growing as a business.

Where were you when you came up with the idea for your business or discovered what you wanted to do?

In terms of my acting career: I went to see a show at UCB (Upright Citizen's Brigade) Theatre almost ten years ago, by myself, because my roommate at the time told me she thought I would like it. I sat there, completely in awe. I have never felt that way before. I knew in that moment that there was no turning back—comedy was the thing.

Name a woman (or women), past or present, whom you admire or look up to.

My mom. She never went to school for art, but you walk into her studio (talk about workspaces) and you are just overcome with a sense of joy and play. She used to sell pottery at craft shows when I was a kid, and it was such a fun experience to be there with her. My mom is also deaf, but she has a cochlear implant. You would never know, though, as she is so resilient and has never made it an issue for herself, but it's something I know she has to deal with. She has such a presence and unique spirit. I always look up to her . . . even though she's a little smaller than me.

"Confidence is mandatory!"

Julia Rothman

Illustrator,
Designer, Author
Brooklyn, NY

What did you want to be when you were a child?

When I was young I really wanted to be a dancer. I took classes four times a week. Then I went through puberty and gained curves and it seemed less likely a possibility. Art was my second choice!

In moments of self-doubt or adversity, how do you build yourself back up?

My mom has always been my cheerleader:

You can do anything you want, Julia! Anything!

She also has a very entrepreneurial spirit:

You could sell that!

What is your favorite thing about your workspace?

I can make a mess and it doesn't matter!

What tool, object, or ritual could you not live without in your workday?

A run in Prospect Park

What is your personal or professional motto?

CONFIDENCE IS MANDATORY!

What does success mean to you?

Being able to do whatever projects I want without worrying about what it will cost me or how easy it is to accomplish.

If you were given $100 million, would you run your business any differently? How so?

I would do ~~more~~ only pro-bono work for good causes and hire people to help me! That's a lot of money!

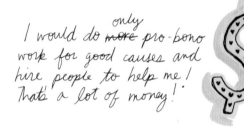

Name a fear or professional challenge that keeps you up at night.

I get really worried about going out of style. Or, not challenging myself to try new things that help me grow as an artist.

What quotation or saying inspires and motivates you to be yourself and do what you love?

" I WANT TO FEEL MY LIFE WHILE I'M IN IT. "
— Meryl Streep

Knowing what you know now, what would you have done differently when you were first starting out?

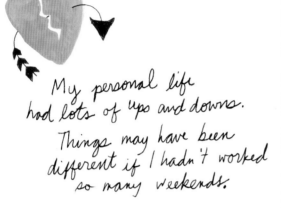

My personal life had lots of ups and downs. Things may have been different if I hadn't worked so many weekends.

Which of your traits are you most proud of?

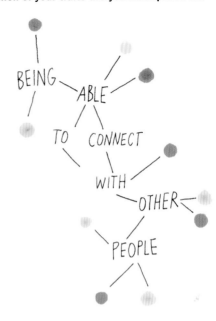

BEING ABLE TO CONNECT WITH OTHER PEOPLE

What's the first thing you do every morning to start your day on the right foot?

Eat a real breakfast and listen to WNYC to hear what's happening in the world.

If you were magically given three more hours per day, what would you do with them?

Draw more—just for fun!

Name a woman (or women), past or present, whom you admire or look up to.

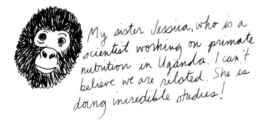

My sister Jessica, who is a scientist working on primate nutrition in Uganda. I can't believe we are related. She is doing incredible studies!

What does the world need more of? Less of?

LESS SCAREDY-CATS
MORE RISK-TAKERS

> "The world needs your voice, so stop trying to fit someone else's idea of who you are. Make them look you dead in the eye; make them know you."

Danielle Henderson

Writer, Editor
New York, NY

What did you want to be when you were a child?

I found a fourth-grade project a few years ago, and I had written down that I wanted to be a poet, professional baseball player, singer, Harvard graduate, and construction worker. I have accomplished absolutely zero of these things, but I applaud the ambition of my younger self.

What characteristic do you most admire in other creative women?

We share resources. It's very rare that I meet a creative woman who isn't eager to bring other women along with her, and I'm a big proponent of sharing the wealth.

What does success mean to you?

How often I can say "yes!" enthusiastically.

What is your favorite thing about your workspace?

It's multifunctional, and since it's only a corner of my tiny New York apartment, it's all killer, no filler.

What is the biggest sacrifice you've made in your career/line of work?

I inadvertently sacrificed some relationships by just not being available; I know I won't get back that time with friends and people I love.

If you were given $100 million, would you run your business any differently? How so?

I'd have a lot more "meetings" from the top of the Eiffel Tower. There's good Wi-Fi up there, right?

Has learning from a mistake ever led you to success?

The biggest mistake I've made as a freelance writer is saying yes to too many projects. I grew up poor and have no one to fall back on; it's entirely up to me to earn a living, and I used to panic about not having enough work. There were a couple of weeks where I stayed awake until four a.m. working, only to wake up at eight a.m. and be back at it, and I legitimately felt like I was going insane. I cried about every assignment, and since I pride myself on not missing deadlines, I was too afraid to ask my editors for help. I've never turned in sloppier work or felt more defeated. After I recovered, I decided that as strange as it sounded, it made more sense for me to take larger projects for more money instead of smaller projects that I worked on daily for smaller paychecks. It still scares the shit out of me sometimes, but it's a decision that helps me work smarter.

Name a fear or professional challenge that keeps you up at night.

I worry that I'm going to get marginalized. I love writing about race, gender, and class, but sometimes it prevents people from seeing that I'm capable of writing about a lot of different topics.

What is your personal or professional motto?

Give yourself permission. I used to think that I didn't have the credentials to do creative work professionally, and I talked myself out of it for years.

Which of your traits are you most proud of?

I'm very funny. And exceedingly humble!

In moments of self-doubt or adversity, how do you build yourself back up?

I like to call a friend wailing and *really* freak them out; then, when we're both spiraling out of control emotionally, I ask them to remind me that I've gotten through this before and will again. That, and stay off Twitter.

What quotation or saying inspires and motivates you to be yourself and do what you love?

It's actually an entire poem by Mary Oliver called "Wild Geese"; so beautiful and thoughtful, and it reminds me that I'm part of a wild, vast world. But my go-to motivation is something my grandmother used to say: "I wish a mutha****ah *would.*" My grandma is tiny and terrifying, and I like to think that there's no obstacle I can't scare out of my way. I learned from the best.

What would you tell yourself ten to twenty years ago that you wish you knew then?

The world needs your voice, so stop trying to fit someone else's idea of who you are. Make them look you dead in the eye; make them know you.

What tool, object, or ritual could you not live without in your workday?

I write out a lot of my ideas longhand before I type them up, and I love Muji 0.38 mm pens. The nib is the perfect width for scratching and furiously trying to outrun your brain before you lose your idea entirely.

Never go with
a hippie
✕ to the ✕
second location

Lord loves a
working man
Don't trust
whitey
See a doctor
and get rid
of it

who's house?

LOIS LANE
GIRL FRIEND

I AM CURIOUS *BLACK!*

Hey Girl.
WHEREVER
BOOKS
ARE SOLD

FEMINIST
RYAN GOSLING

Feminist Theory
from Your
Favorite Sensitive
Movie Dude

FEMINISTRYANGOSLING.TUMBLR.COM

> "If I am feeling self-doubt, I always try to think of myself as a kid. What I liked as a child is always a good barometer for what is good for me."

Joana Avillez

Illustrator
New York, NY

What did you want to be when you were a child?

I recently found a diary entry from when I was seven or eight that states, "When I grow up, I want to be a children's book illustrator, an interior designer, and an actress." I think the latter two actually fit into the idea of being an illustrator: I often have to embody and visualize someone within a space and draw it. I also just wanted to keep drawing with my dad.

What characteristic do you most admire in other creative women?

Women seem often to innately have this propensity to make sure everyone "is okay"—I do it too. I like, within reason, when I can tell that a woman is really thinking of caring for herself as a priority. She is not bending over backward to please. It can be very distracting to cater to everyone around you. However, I'm sure that all goes out the window when you have kids.

What does success mean to you?

Success is twofold: On the one hand there is the pleasure and triumph and freedom of being able to step back, and in my case realize that I am making a living actually drawing. I like to imagine what nine-year-old me would think of twenty-nine-year-old me. And then the other half of success is feeling that you are getting somewhere with your work. That you are progressing and getting closer and closer to that thing that really feels like you. From what I've gathered, I think it is, thankfully, a lifelong chase.

What is your favorite thing about your workspace?

I live and work in the same space. It is a loft that used to be my dad's office, where he ran a small journal on art and politics called *Lusitania*. I love that it has elements of him in it—from framework to teakettle. I also really love the high ceilings.

Has learning from a mistake ever led you to success?

I have followed many different avenues of what I thought was an obvious marriage of drawing and writing. For a few months I tried making *New Yorker* cartoons. They were *terrible*! I went every week and submitted them in person, as is the custom, to the cartoon editor. Getting rejected week after week (as is also the custom for newbies), I realized later, was actually incredibly freeing—I felt so much less precious with things I made and it released me from a fear of being rejected. This didn't work? Try again and keep following your nose.

In moments of self-doubt or adversity, how do you build yourself back up?

If I am feeling self-doubt, I always try to think of myself as a kid. Perhaps it sounds obvious and cheesy, but what I liked as a child is always a good barometer for what is good for me. If you can go back to those initial moments of self-discovery and what drew you to what you love, you can get back to the unfettered root of it. If I think of the hours I spent drawing by myself, creating worlds, the afternoons poring over books on my parents' sofa, the prick of the things that really interested me, I am right back there without any of the contemporary hubbub.

What would you tell yourself ten to twenty years ago that you wish you knew then?

You can make a job for yourself that isn't as literal as options at a career day. There are so many nuances within each world, within each profession.

What quotation inspires and motivates you to be yourself and do what you love?

In a letter to me at summer camp, my dad drew a cute and tiny monster/animal character, with a word bubble that said: THE THING IS—BE YOURSELF! It is so simple, but so perfect and true. After my dad passed away I got it engraved on a ring, so I'll look at that if I'm feeling low, and it cheers me up and makes me feel cared for.

What is your no-fail go-to when you need inspiration or to get out of a creative rut?

Call my mom and complain.

What's the first thing you do every morning to start your day on the right foot?

Having a dog gives me no choice but to bound out of the house very early for a long walk. The life of an illustrator can be sedentary, but my dog, Pepe, has made that impossible.

"Joy eclipses pain."

Alice Randall and Caroline Randall-Williams

Writers, Food Activists
Morgantown, WV

What did you want to be when you were a child?

Alice: When I was in the seventh grade, I read *In the Shadow of Man* and was smitten with the independence, intelligence, and adventures of Jane Goodall. I wrote my shero an aerogram addressed "Jane Goodall, Gombe Stream, Tanzania," declaring my intent to become an anthropologist. A year later I got a handwritten letter back from Goodall stating that I should come one day and study with her at Stanford. In 1977 I landed at Harvard and enrolled in a course called something along the lines of "Man the Peculiar Primate" taught by renowned anthropologist Irven DeVore—who hated Goodall. About the same time, I was introduced to the work of Zora Neale Hurston, a black novelist who had begun life as an anthropologist. I am still fascinated by human culture and the details and varieties of human life, but soon my passion for anthropology morphed into an interest in writing novels that explore human behavior. I loved the idea of walking in Zora Neale Hurston's footsteps.

What characteristic do you most admire in other creative women?

A: The willingness to see what is missing in the world and create it rather than lament it.

Caroline: There are women who have committed their work to witnessing, and to truth telling. The vulnerability and fortitude required to make art that speaks up for itself and out for others, that fights for both personal and social justice always has my highest regard; I find it awe-inspiring.

What does success mean to you?

A: As a novelist I define success as speaking for those who cannot speak for themselves, often the dead and the dispossessed. More women than we commonly acknowledge have been stripped of their public voice. I seek to see, understand, and narrate untold but necessary stories. As a food activist I define success as one less person getting diabetes a year later because of my work. As a mother I define success as raising a daughter who has never had to worry about whether or not I loved and respected her.

C: Success, to me, would be a life lived, and lived well, by my pen. Whether it's wielded to write poetry or to write cookbooks, I want to move, engage, and sustain people through my work, in a way that also allows me to sustain myself.

What is the biggest sacrifice you've made in your career/line of work?

C: My privacy. The stories and struggles that are hardest to tell are, I often find, the ones that really ought to be told. I'm told that some people are able to keep their private lives out of their creative work, but I am not one of them. Whatever feels most important or helpful to share, I'll share, regardless of how personal.

Mother and daughter Alice Randall (right)
and Caroline Randall-Williams

What is your favorite thing about your workspace?

A: My favorite thing about my workspace is that it is cocreated. I enjoy the rare privilege of writing books with my daughter.

C: Its hybridity. Working at a dining room table can mean so many things throughout a day, throughout a week, throughout a life. Having books in an eating room, having food in a writing room, allows and invites me, even, to wear so many different hats. Food and writing have always and will always go together in my life, but this space facilitates and enhances that relationship in a wonderful way.

In moments of self-doubt or adversity, how do you build yourself back up?

A: I remember how far I've come. I remember that joy eclipses pain. I started off life as a severely abused child. Before my mother died she acknowledged that the expected outcome of her abuse was that I would either be dead or in jail. But my mother was not my only influence: I had a grandmother, aunties, and, from the time I entered kindergarten, best friends. Anita, Leslie, Mimi. Joan. And now my daughter, Caroline. When I'm down, I think about me as those women see me. This helps me remember who I am. Always. The early friendships, a memory of swinging high in the trees creating words for the distances, and the last miracle friendship, with my daughter, sustain me. And I dance around my bedroom all by myself listening to my favorite songs.

C: Having my mother in my corner is a pretty extraordinary resource.

What is your personal or professional motto?

C: Deep down, I'm a Shakespeare girl through and through, so I'd have to say, "Once more unto the breach, dear friends," from *Henry V*. I love the idea of relentless pursuit of achievement.

What does the world need more of? Less of?

A: The world needs more optimism and generosity. We need less narrow-mindedness.

C: The world needs more teachers, and more money allocated toward paying them.

What would you tell yourself ten to twenty years ago that you wish you knew then?

A: Pay attention to the contracts.

C: I would tell my seventeen-year-old self, "The things you don't think are beautiful are in fact beautiful. And what's more, you will know it, and be happy."

Name a woman (or women), past or present, whom you admire or look up to.

A: There are so many . . . but one who stands above the others is Harriet Tubman. I've known about her since my earliest days. What touched me from the first is what touches me now: that after gaining her own freedom, she risked it again and again, went back down South to help free others. Her unselfishness, her courage, her competence, her imagination. I love it all.

C: Well, it would have to be a three-way tie between my mother, Maya Angelou, and Queen Elizabeth I.

**What is your personal
or professional motto?**

A: Do the hard right thing.
Be three times as good
and have what you want.
If you don't know where
something is, you don't
know where it isn't.

> **"The ability to adapt what you're doing and truly self-evaluate is so important."**

Anna Bond

Artist, Designer
Winter Park, FL

What did you want to be when you were a child?

I remember a long list of things I wanted to be—a teacher, mother, architect, writer, social worker, artist. That last one, artist, always seemed to be the constant and eventually became my focus. It just took me a long time to realize what that could mean as a career. No one was telling me in grade school that I could be a graphic designer or product developer, which is a bit of a shame. I think it's important to expose children to as many types of careers as possible at a young age.

What was the best piece of business advice you were given when you were starting out?

One of the best pieces of advice I've received is to always be flexible. The ability to adapt what you're doing and truly self-evaluate is so important in order to constantly fine-tune your business and keep it moving in the right direction.

Has learning from a mistake ever led you to success?

Constantly learning what works and what doesn't in the market is moving us toward success. Over time I have learned which designs sell better than others on store shelves. I've championed products that I thought would be a huge success, only to find out they were complete duds. That's always the best opportunity to learn.

At what point in your life did you first learn about your field of work? What called you to it?

Looking back, it was a process and many different loves coming together. When I was little, I loved stamps and stationery; I remember being seven or eight years old and telling my dad I wanted to start a logo company called Anna's Logo Shoppe. I loved magazine layouts, album covers, and painting. I eventually studied graphic design in college and ended up freelancing. I learned I wanted to work for myself and had the drive to build something on my own. All that led me to start a stationery company, Rifle Paper Co., and a brand where I could do all those things I fell in love with over the years.

In your opinion, what are the top three things someone should consider before starting a business?

1. Is it viable, original, and needed in the market?
2. Do I have the drive and discipline to see it through and do what it takes to be successful?
3. Am I willing to step back and objectively evaluate, adapt, and adjust what I am doing?

Knowing what you know now, what would you have done differently when you were first starting out?

I would have reached out for help a bit more and tried to find a mentor. We didn't know anyone in the industry and didn't have anyone to lean on for general advice. We learned along the way, but I think we would have made our lives a bit easier had we tried to find someone to do that.

> "We all get knocked down—what matters is resilience. The ability to learn from a stumble, regain momentum, and reinvent, if necessary."

Dominique Browning

Author, Activist
Little Compton, RI

What did you want to be when you were a child?

A spy: as in *Get Smart*. An astronaut: I wanted to live on another planet. A boss: Why was my mother in charge of *my* life? Never again.

What characteristic do you most admire in other creative women?

Resilience. We all get knocked down—what matters is resilience. The ability to learn from a stumble, regain momentum, and reinvent, if necessary. For that reason, I loathe whining and whiners. Just get going.

What does success mean to you?

My definition of success cascades up, I think. First, I have to support myself, so having a job means I'm successful. Bottom line. Then, the job should be a good one: meaning, I'm always learning. Then, the job should be soul-satisfying. Then, success means I am helping to make the world a better place—for someone, somewhere, whether by entertaining or diverting a reader, or fighting big polluters. The bar gets higher. Success might never be attained. But then again, I also feel extremely successful if I've weeded the iris bed, or made a tomato galette. Maybe I define success as simply doing things I don't think I am capable of doing.

What is the biggest sacrifice you've made in your career/line of work?

Time with my children. I must confess that there were plenty of days when it was a relief to walk away from the endless tedium of child rearing. (Only to walk into the endless tedium of writer rearing.) But looking back, I do feel sharply the lost time. But I'd probably feel that way even if they had been glued to my side all day. I hasten to add that my children are *very* glad that I had a job other than raising them.

In moments of self-doubt or adversity, how do you build yourself back up?

Ah, see, resilience: the key to life. The seven-step process:

1. Let yourself boil over with fury, and vent, rage, curse, rain down wrath, and tear out your hair. (But try not to do it publicly. And certainly not online.)
2. Let yourself mourn. Setbacks are sad. Maybe even depressing—but don't confuse the two. Let yourself feel the sadness of loss.
3. Get moving. You don't want that sadness to tip into a paralyzing depression. So get out and take a walk, several times a day. Feel the air move against your cheeks. Feel forward momentum.
4. Learn to ask for help. Most successful people get there by being strong and independent. We help others. It is harder to learn to ask when we need help—and to realize that admitting it is not a sign of weakness. It is a sign of respect for what others can contribute to your life.
5. Turn your thinking upside down: That wasn't a setback. It was an opportunity to re-create.
6. Know fear, and honor it. When you feel fear, that's when you are growing.
7. Stop negative thinking: Just stop. Force it. Including the arrogance of thinking everything was your fault. You aren't really in control of much. Bad luck happens. Now what are you going to do about it? That's the really interesting—and even thrilling—part.

> "To me success means having the freedom to do whatever you want with your day."

Ana Serrano

Artist
Los Angeles, CA

What did you want to be when you were a child?

I always knew I wanted to do something creative. At different times I remember wanting to be an architect, a fashion designer, a photographer. I was curious about it all.

What was the best piece of business advice you were given when you were starting out?

I was told, "Make whatever you want and think about the application later." That advice was really freeing for me. I used to get caught up in thinking about the process of making work and of the result. Once I started making work that came naturally to me, I found my voice, and found my audience.

What is your favorite thing about your workspace?

That it doesn't matter if I get paint on the floors, or anywhere, really. It makes working less stressful when I can be messy.

In moments of self-doubt or adversity, how do you build yourself back up?

Talking through it with friends who are also artists. I feel lucky to have many friends I can rely on to talk about the ups and downs about art making. We all go through the same struggles and have the same fears, but being able to talk about them and work through them together makes things easier.

What quotation or saying inspires and motivates you to be yourself and do what you love?

"Life is short." It puts life into perspective quickly for me, it makes me grateful to be alive and to be healthy, and it reminds me to focus on the really important things, like making sure I'm happy and spending time with loved ones.

Knowing what you know now, what would you have done differently when you were first starting out?

There were many times I put things off because I didn't know how to do them. I wish I would have asked someone for help.

Which of your traits are you most proud of?

I'm most proud of being able to stay focused and work fast under pressure.

What is your no-fail go-to when you need inspiration or to get out of a creative rut?

When I'm out running errands, I'll take the long way home and drive through streets I've never been on. The city is always an inspiration. Also, I go to the library and look at art books. I love discovering new things this way.

Name a woman (or women), past or present, whom you admire or look up to.

Ray Eames. I love the extent to which art and design infiltrated her day-to-day life.

What does success mean to you?

To me success means having the freedom to do whatever you want with your day.

CASHED

KICK IT
CRICKET

EL SABIO CALLA
EL INTELIGENTE DISCUTE
EL IDIOTA GRITA
ENTONCES QUIEN SOY
AHORITA

"Grow organically. Don't get ahead of yourself."

Eileen Fisher

Fashion Designer,
Entrepreneur
Irvington, NY

What did you want to be when you were a child?
I wanted to be a dancer. Though I never took a dance class.

What was the best piece of business advice you were given when you were starting out?
Grow organically. Don't get ahead of yourself. If you create a product that people truly enjoy and benefit from, profitability will always follow.

What does success mean to you?
Happy customers: finding women who love our clothes. Having a positive impact in the world: sustainability work with other initiatives like women's leadership. Helping others: employees, other female entrepreneurs, girls' leadership.

Name a fear or professional challenge that keeps you up at night.
Maintaining the essence of the brand. How we as a company define profitability and adapt a sustainable business model. A real fear of mine is public speaking—anything from speaking in front of a small group of people to giving a speech to a large audience.

Has learning from a mistake ever led you to success?
In the early days I chose to use only French terry as the main fabric. It was a minor disaster. I learned that if I broadened my fabric choices in the same silhouettes, it would expand my collection—the business exploded after that. All the challenges I have faced are just new opportunities presenting themselves.

Name your greatest success (or something you're most proud of) in your business experiences.
My core design concept is still relevant after thirty years. I am also incredibly proud of the sustainability work my company has accomplished and of building a company with purpose. I also love to see the older pieces that come through our Green Eileen program. It is nice to see that the clothing lasts and is still meaningful and relevant.

Knowing what you know now, what would you have done differently when you were first starting out?
I would have been less driven—I would have tried to be calmer and take it a little slower; tried to make more conscious decisions. I would have liked to have put myself at the center earlier and kept my own life as more of a priority.

What does the world need more of? Less of?

The world needs more love, happiness, and joy, and less stuff. You still need stuff, but just the *right* stuff.

What is your no-fail go-to when you need inspiration or to get out of a creative rut?
I have a purpose chair that I like to spend time in. I also like to write. For me, taking time to just ramble-write in my journal for pages at a time energizes me. If I write it down, I can see through the mess and gain clarity in what I need to do and the next steps.

> "I am proud to be an out, queer woman of color in an industry where there are so few people like me."

Jasika Nicole

Actor, Maker
Los Angeles, CA

What did you want to be when you were a child?

When I was a kid, I alternated between wanting to be a commercial jingle writer and a marine biologist. My family wasn't able to afford music lessons when I was young, so even though I loved the cheap electric organ I got for my birthday, I never learned how to actually play it. And I was in middle school when I realized that to be a marine biologist you had to spend a fair amount of time in the water, and since I have always been really uncomfortable in the ocean, that dream was dashed too. But taking theater classes in school was free, and I realized pretty quickly that being onstage was something I was good at. By the time I graduated from high school, "actor" had become the thing I wanted to be.

What characteristic do you most admire in other creative women?

Their ability to say no. Saying no wasn't something I realized I had the power to do till I was in my twenties, and if I am honest, it's still not something I am always completely comfortable with. But it is one of the most empowering things I have learned to do.

What is your favorite thing about your workspace?

Oh, boy. I have so *many* workspaces! And maybe that's my favorite thing about them—the fact that I am not confined to one area; this house as a whole is a workspace for me. It's the main reason that I wanted to move to Los Angeles instead of back to New York City after I worked in Vancouver for four years—I wanted to have space. And I have taken full advantage of it—without all this space I wouldn't have been able to learn half the skills I now have.

If you were given $100 million, would you run your business any differently? How so?

I am usually at the mercy of other people deciding when and how and in what capacity I work. So with all that money, I would probably start creating my *own* acting work—finding scripts and producing dynamic, original content with a diverse group of actors and writers would be incredibly exciting. But with all that money I would also want to expand my business to involve creating some nonprofits for LGBTQ and at-risk youth in the community. I think there can never be enough programs geared toward those demographics, and one of my dreams has been to start an organization that teaches kids and teens how to create things with their hands, with an emphasis on reusing and repurposing.

Name a fear or professional challenge that keeps you up at night.

My biggest fear in my line of work as an actor is that my sexuality inhibits me from getting more roles. Obviously the color of my skin keeps me from being considered for a lot of work, since the majority of leading roles cast in U.S. film and television are for white actors. But I think the truth about homophobic casting practices in Hollywood is a bit more evasive, and since it's nothing I can prove, I can only worry myself over it and find solace in other actor friends who have the same fears. I am proud to be an out, queer woman of color in an industry where there are so few people like me, so the fear isn't regarding the fact that I am out—the fear is that I am actively participating in an industry that doesn't value the diverse narratives of the very people who help give it its power.

In moments of self-doubt or adversity, how do you build yourself back up?

When I experience moments of adversity or self-doubt that are tied into my career as an actor, I usually try to focus on all the other things that I do in my life that bring me joy, the other things that I am good at. I may not have been young enough or glamorous enough or dramatic enough for the role, but damn it, I *made* this gorgeous dress!

What does the world need more of?

I think the world needs more people with hobbies. This is easier said than done—so many hobbies require things like extra time or extra money or extra space, and those are luxuries for the majority of adults living in this country. But I think the effects of incorporating activities and experiences in our lives that bring us joy can be incredibly beneficial to our sense of pride and happiness.

"Lead with love."

Mary Verdi-Fletcher

Dancer, Choreographer
Cleveland, OH

What did you want to be when you were a child?

I wanted to be a dancer and follow in my mother's footsteps for as long as I can remember. I believe I was three years old when I started telling people that I wanted to be a dancer even though I was in a wheelchair.

What characteristic do you most admire in other creative women?

I admire the inner strength that seems to exude from women who dare to dream and succeed in their quest.

What is your favorite thing about your workspace?

Ninety percent of the time it is filled with music.

Has learning from a mistake ever led you to success?

In my early years I was so afraid of losing the company, I would depend on those who I thought had more knowledge and artistry than I did. I would allow them to feed their egos and to take advantage of the organization and me. I hired the wrong people to help run the organization. I equate it to an abusive marriage, in which the one partner doesn't realize they are being suppressed. I managed to rise out of that situation by letting the abusers go and took control over my life and the direction of the organization. This decision was the best of my life!

In moments of self-doubt or adversity, how do you build yourself back up?

Basically I give myself a good talking-to and say, if you want to change it, you have to take control and just roll up your sleeves and do it!

What quotation or saying inspires and motivates you to be yourself and do what you love?

Ironically, I often think of what my mother taught me to say when I was little. When people asked about my disability, she would say, "Tell them, 'I'm not handicapped, I'm Mary!'" At the time I did not understand, but today I know she meant for people to see me, not my disability.

Which of your traits are you most proud of?

My emotional strength.

What is your personal or professional motto?

Lead with love. If you do that, then most of your decisions are made for the right reasons.

What does the world need more of?

I think especially our young people need to think more about service than self.

Where were you when you came up with the idea for your business or discovered what you wanted to do?

The idea to start the Dancing Wheels Company came about when I first entered a dance competition with a nondisabled partner. I went out onstage before two thousand people as the only wheelchair dance competitor and took the national judge and audience by surprise. We ended up being runners-up to be on a national TV show called *Dance Fever*. From there we received national attention, and the rest is history!

What tool, object, or ritual could you not live without in your workday?

I pray every day. I have a special prayer to St. Teresa, and it is truly better than any mantra.

"I'm strictly no bullshit. I'm the most fun and easygoing when simplicity and goodness rule the roost."

Randi Brookman Harris

Prop Stylist
Brooklyn, NY

What did you want to be when you were a child?

I always wanted to be an artist. I liked the exercise of tinkering around and seeing what happened when I "did art," but I didn't realize until I became a stylist that I wasn't actually a "maker." I wanted to oversee and experiment and put together, and see how things looked together and layer things. When I started living on my own after studying graphic design in art school, I started tinkering with interior still life. And I wanted to live with arrangements, constantly reworking the vignettes in my apartment. I think if I had known about styling before I actually did, I would have skipped all these crucial (to me) steps in experimentation for years and years. I'm actually grateful I didn't stumble upon it until I was ready to do it—until I had all the foundational steps and layers and layers of just figuring out stuff.

What is your favorite thing about your workspace?

I love working at home because time alone in my home gives me so much peace. I don't have a true dedicated working space, so I sit at our dining table, and I usually have a traveling stack of papers, but after a job I dump all my notes right into the trash! That is the *best*. I wonder if I had a desk that I didn't have to clear every time we have a meal, whether I would hang on to stuff. I save receipts and all that kind of practical filing detritus in an accordion folder, but otherwise, I'm kind of paperless and mobile.

My other workspace—technically—is the entire city, and I love that I know where to go to get the most obscure stuff, and that I have been discovering special places in New York City for nearly two decades. I find the discovery to be the most fun I have working. I'm all my friends' go-to for helping to source anything. The weirder, the better.

What does success mean to you?

Being the prop stylist on everyone's short list. I love when a client calls me back and especially when they work around my schedule to get me on a project because they can't imagine someone else doing it.

Name the biggest overall lesson you've learned in running a business.

- Trust is earned.
- Hard work means different things to different people.
- Creativity and concept is subjective.
- Contracts need to be ironclad. They are also annoying.
- Chasing money is the worst.

Has learning from a mistake ever led you to success?

Every time I've been burned by some dumb happenstance on a job, I add a new clause to my contract.

Which of your traits are you most proud of?

I'm strictly no bullshit. I'm the most fun and easygoing when simplicity and goodness rule the roost.

In moments of self-doubt or adversity, how do you build yourself back up?

Indulge in chocolate. Wait it out.

At what point in your life did you first learn about your field of work? What called you to it?

I had no idea about prop styling as an industry until I was three years out of art school, having graduated with a BFA in graphic design. (Incidentally, I didn't know about graphic design until I had already been accepted as a transfer student for fine art at the School of Visual Arts my sophomore year. I just took that plunge with the faith of a nineteen-year-old.) Once out in the world practicing my trade, I was already unsure about graphic design when I attended a lecture panel given by the editors of *Martha Stewart Living*. Learning about what styling was that evening, I felt like I was being rescued from the wrong fit to the right place. I realized I had always practiced styling without ever knowing it was a job that existed. I floated home, my mind racing a zillion miles an hour. I contacted the style director from the lecture the very next day. She hired me; I knew she would. There was no other option in my mind. Working at Martha Stewart for those next six years was the best styling boot camp and finishing school for good taste. I was exposed to the best of everything and the most talented people.

What does the world need more of? Less of?

More beauty, kindness, humor, understanding. Less judgment, mediocrity.

What is your personal or professional motto?

Say no to things you don't want to do, kindly and politely. And give a widely known enthusiastic *yes* to the things you do want to do.

HARPER'S

BAZAAR

please do come to us for Christmas . . .

I understand you sell partridges in pear trees . . .

. . . brandy, cream, nutmeg—and what?

I finally found Blitzen . . .

. . . after Candlelight Service . . .

but George always plays Santa like King Lear . . .

. . . yes, the goose came—but it's alive . . .

60 Cents

December 1958

"Everything has a solution."

Llubav Choy Duerr

Artist, Illustrator
Brooklyn, NY

What did you want to be when you were a child?

A modern dancer. As a kid I dreamed of joining the *Fame* dance school like on the '80s TV show.

What characteristic do you most admire in other creative women?

I really admire those women who can be creative not only in making things, but also in running a business. It is so difficult to do both, but when you're a sole proprietor of a small company, it's essential.

What is the biggest sacrifice you've made in your career/line of work?

Quitting my job and putting my dream of having my own textile collection on indefinite hold to have kids and raise them full-time.

Has learning from a mistake ever led you to success?

I started a custom-order wedding-ring-pillow business after a friend asked me to make her one. Many orders followed and it was wonderful at first, but then with time they became hard on my hands. They were labor-intensive and I couldn't make them fast enough. I found myself consumed with back-and-forth e-mails with clients and at times lost business because it was not a situation where I had stock set aside to pack and ship at any given moment. I later learned how important it is to write things down to have a good guideline to follow. This difficult experience led me to seek out a more productive business in painting stationery where I'm able to wholesale and ship orders faster.

Name a fear or professional challenge that keeps you up at night.

I am afraid to one day get up and not be able to paint because of too much pain in my hands, or worse, be unable to move my hands. I was diagnosed with psoriatic arthritis in 2014 and it's been a terrible ordeal—especially learning how to manage the pain. It's an illness that could eventually destroy my joints.

In moments of self-doubt or adversity, how do you build yourself back up?

I find great comfort in prayer and also speaking to my husband and mother. It's soothing to hear both their thoughts and opinions.

What does the world need more of? Less of?

More compassion, less hate.

What would you tell yourself ten to twenty years ago that you wish you knew then?

Everything has a solution.

Name a woman (or women), past or present, whom you admire or look up to.

Frida Kahlo is someone I strongly admire. She had a traffic accident early in her life but that didn't stop her from expressing herself through her paintings. She had a strong will, courage, and passion.

Mary Lambert

Musician
Amherst, MA

What did you want to be when you were a child?

Like a lot of kids, I went through phases of ideal career paths. When asked at age three what I wanted to be, I simply responded, "Space." Another time I replied, "A doctor!" My mom asked what kind of doctor, and after a long pause, I said, "A Doctor Seuss." Around seven or eight, I had finally settled on being a singing, dancing waitress.

What was the best piece of business advice you were given when you were starting out?

I glean a lot of information purely by observation. Especially when I was starting out, I was a sponge. I looked at an artist I respected and tried to figure out how they got to where they were. One thing I started to gather from artists I looked up to was that they never felt like anything was beneath them. Before they had an agent, they booked their own shows, their own tours, they worked part-time jobs to supplement their dream. They packaged their merch, lugged their own gear across town, learned how to record their own vocals, and, most admirably, paid out their band before they paid themselves. In that way, they were directly connected to all points of their business. All the artists I respected never felt entitled to success or money.

What is your favorite thing about your workspace?
Because my workspace is in my home, I'm able to be close to my partner and my cat, and work on my garden or cook a healthy snack when I take a break. It all feels really balanced. Sometimes when I'm working on a song, I'll notice that the cat has moved onto the couch to hear the piano. As soon as he climbs up to the edge and starts purring, I know I'm onto something good!

Has learning from a mistake ever led you to success?
I was involved in a very successful collaboration that earned a lot of money and a lot of notoriety. I felt so fortunate and lucky to be a part of that song, but because I was so young in my career and had no idea what was going on, I didn't realize that I had signed away all my royalties. It definitely still haunts me. I am grateful in some way, though, because I now know how to *never* treat another writer or musician. Everyone I work with gets their fair share, and is treated with kindness both in business and in friendship. Another thing that came out of that unfortunate situation was that I had to figure out how to capitalize on that collaboration, which I did very successfully. I lost in one way, but definitely gained in another.

In moments of self-doubt or adversity, how do you build yourself back up?
I don't know how many times I've heard that it's important to your growth as an artist or business-person to "get out of your comfort zone," but I find there's been a very clear difference between stretching my own boundaries when I feel safe and grounded and someone telling me to do something I'm not comfortable with. To get myself out of those situations, I've learned how to be direct and assertive. To say, "I understand that you think x is a good idea, but this is my business decision/creative work and I want it to be like y. Maybe someday down the road I will come to a place where I feel like x is what I want to do, but I'm

not there right now, and I need you to respect and honor my voice and decision-making."

I wish there was a different phrase like, "Get out of your comfort zone, but if you start crying a lot and feeling bad about yourself and your art, that is also not good, and you should go back to what you feel like doing and makes you happy," but I guess it would be difficult to put that on a motivational poster.

Name your greatest success (or something you're most proud of) in your business experiences.
I remember the day before I performed at the Grammys with Madonna, Macklemore, and Ryan Lewis. It was completely surreal. When I found out "Same Love" was nominated for Song of the Year, I lost my mind, but when I was told we were also performing it for millions of people alongside Madonna, while Queen Latifah officiated thirty marriages onstage, I completely broke down. Not only was it an incredible opportunity for me as an artist to share the stage with such iconic performers, but it meant everything to me as a lesbian in the gay community. I thought about seventeen-year-old me, unsure about coming out and having very few role models to look up to. I thought about how much watching something like that on TV would have meant to me, and that in 2014, maybe somewhere, there was another seventeen-year-old kid trying to sort through the madness, and maybe seeing our performance made it a little bit easier. Years prior, I wanted so badly to contribute in the gay marriage fight but didn't really know how. That day, I was able to stand proudly as a lesbian, singing a song I wrote in three hours about universal love, and I was embraced by the world. I will never forget that day.

What's your favorite thing to come home to after a long day of work?
It is a ritual in our house to take a walk or bike ride at sunset. It signifies the end of the workday for both me and my partner, Michelle, who is also an artist. We take a lengthy walk or ride, debrief about our workdays, and then cook dinner together. It is something I look forward to every day.

What is your no-fail go-to when you need inspiration or to get out of a creative rut?

I love going to shows or spoken-word performances, especially when I've hit a wall. Passion is definitely contagious.

> "Ever since becoming a mother, I am mostly motivated by the desire to set an example for my daughters. I want them to see that they have a mom who truly loves what she does."

Joy Cho
Designer, Blogger
Los Angeles, CA

What did you want to be when you were a child?

A cheerleader, a botanist, a geneticist, a journalist, and a stunt double.

What was the best piece of business advice you were given when you were starting out?

"Who says you can't do it?"

What is your favorite thing about your workspace?

I was able to design and furnish it however I wanted. Unlike my home, I didn't have to worry about my husband's taste or super-practical things like childproofing. It's sort of like my own personal colorful wonderland.

Has learning from a mistake ever led you to success?

There have been times in my life and business where things were slow and money was really tight. And when you feel the pressure of not being able to pay your bills, you start to take more work that you might not always enjoy. Not every project is a dream project, and especially when you're starting out, it's about gaining experience too. But there was one time early in my business that I took a job that was completely not the right fit. I had no interest in the subject matter and took it just because I needed the money. My lack of interest showed in my work, and I got fired from the project. That experience taught me that I really need to be excited for what I am working on and not say yes to everything just because it's a paycheck.

What motivates you to be yourself and do what you love?

Ever since becoming a mother, I am mostly motivated by the desire to set an example for my daughters. I want them to see that they have a mom who created something from nothing, who made her job into what she wanted, and who truly loves what she does. I want them to believe they can make their future career into anything they want to (and that working can be fun too!).

What does the world need more of?

The world needs more positivity and encouragement toward each other . . . not just for those you know and love but toward people you don't know. How good would it make you feel if someone pointed out what a great job you did when they don't even know you?

Which of your traits are you most proud of?

I'm a go-getter. Ninety-five percent of the things I've wanted, careerwise, I have gone after myself. You can't sit there and wait for things to fall into your lap. You're in charge of your life, so go after what you want.

> "I don't see success as a linear rise to money or fame, but rather as a full circle that leads me back home with the things I set out to accomplish."

Bethany Yellowtail

Fashion Designer
Los Angeles, CA

What did you want to be when you were a child?

I wanted to be a basketball player. Where I come from, basketball is god on the reservation. It seemed like the only plausible thing I could do to be successful back then. It wasn't until a high school home-ec teacher saw my creative side that I realized I had a natural skill for designing.

What characteristic do you most admire in other creative women?

I admire their fearlessness. Sometimes it's scary to put your ideas and creations out into public space. I admire creative women who do this unabashedly, and I've learned to be one of them.

In your life and line of work, how do you define success?

I define success as seeing my dreams and goals come to fruition. I don't see success as a linear rise to money or fame, but rather as a full circle that leads me back home with the things I set out to accomplish.

If you were given $100 million, would you run your business any differently? How so?

I would build a manufacturer back home on the Crow Nation and employ my own people. I would bring an entire new economy to my reservation, while providing a space for cultural/traditional arts to thrive. $100 million or not, that's where I will be with my business in the future.

What is the biggest sacrifice you've made in your career/line of work?

Not being with my family or community as much as I'd like to be. I'm from a tribal people, and being away and not being able to participate has been hard. It's been very lonely at times.

Name a fear or professional challenge that keeps you up at night.

Sometimes I fear that I'll have to work for someone else again.

In moments of self-doubt or adversity, how do you build yourself back up?

Prayer. My first instinct when I start stressing is to call home, and I always get the same response: Pray. I was also named "Overcomes Through Faith" on my Crow side and "Sun Road Woman" on my Northern Cheyenne side. Reflecting on those names and the prayerful people who gave them to me is another source of strength for me.

What quotation or saying inspires you and motivates you to be yourself and do what you love?

"Suddenly all my ancestors are behind me. 'Be still,' they say. 'Watch and listen; you are the result of the love of thousands.'"

What would you tell yourself ten or twenty years ago that you wish you knew then?

I would tell my seventeen-year-old self, "It doesn't matter where you come from; you deserve to dream and have the same opportunities anyone else has. You are allowed too."

> "The feeling of connection is a part of my personality and my work, and I am grateful for it."

Rinne Allen

Photographer,
Artist, Author
Athens, GA

What did you want to be when you were a child?

I do not remember having a strong pull toward just one thing when I was little. I actually remember feeling a little bit confused when someone would ask me what I wanted to be when I grew up because I couldn't settle on just one thing.

What characteristic do you most admire in other creative women?

I admire anyone who pursues what they believe in, and I think that to pursue something creative you need an extra dose of curiosity and perseverance. Add in a dash of women's issues (motherhood, work-life balance, etc.) and it makes me really admire not only creative women, but creative women who are also mothers.

What is your favorite thing about your workspace?

I love that my workspace is right next door to my house. I move back and forth between the two throughout the day, crossing through the garden that connects them.

Which of your traits are you most proud of?

I am deeply rooted in my community of Athens, Georgia. I love living in a place that I feel so connected to, that is close to my family, and that is full of so many creative, inspiring, giving people. This feeling of connection is a part of my personality and my work, and I am grateful for it.

What tool, object, or ritual could you not live without in your workday?

Natural light.

What's the first thing you do every morning to start your day on the right foot?

Honestly, my days often begin when my children want them to begin. Therefore, some days I am thrown into the day having not necessarily started it on the right foot. But I have learned that you just have to go with it, and at some point in the day things eventually get on track. If not, there is always tomorrow.

What would you tell yourself ten to twenty years ago that you wish you knew then?

I would tell myself to hang in there, that with age comes experience and with experience comes the confidence to go with what you think is right, in your gut.

> "My definition of success has very little to do with other people's expectations or definitions of success."

Sheila Bridges

Interior Designer
New York, NY

What did you want to be when you were a child?
A veterinarian, because of my fascination with and love of animals.

What does success mean to you?
Success for me both personally and professionally is accomplishing anything I set out to do. My definition of success has very little to do with other people's expectations or definitions of success.

What is your favorite thing about your workspace?
I work from home, so I love the fact that I don't have a commute and can wear pajamas to work some days.

What's the first thing you do every morning to start your day on the right foot?
I walk my two dogs in Central Park.

Has learning from a mistake ever led you to success?

Over the years, I've learned to trust my gut when it comes to people and situations. Many of the relationships (both personal and professional) that have gone awry in my life have because I chose to ignore the signs. Don't be afraid of your own intuitive power as a woman.

Which of your traits are you most proud of?
My ability to creatively problem-solve.

Where were you when you came up with the idea for your business or discovered what you wanted to do?
I was working for an architectural firm in Manhattan, which made me realize that one day I could do the same for myself.

What is your no-fail go-to when you need inspiration or to get out of a creative rut?

Travel is the best way to find inspiration and clear the cobwebs.

> "Nobody knows better what you're capable of than you. Trust yourself. Trust your ideas."

Tina Roth Eisenberg

Graphic Designer,
Entrepreneur
Brooklyn, NY

What did you want to be when you were a child?

For a while I thought I would take over my mother's high-end clothing store, which my grandfather founded. I am glad I didn't. Knowing what I know now, I am certain that the fashion industry wouldn't have been a good fit (pun intended).

What was the best piece of business advice you were given when you were starting out?

Nobody knows better what you're capable of than you. Trust yourself. Trust your ideas. I have a lot of young people asking me for advice, presenting me their ideas for business, thinking I know the ultimate answer to their questions. I always tell them, if you believe, deep inside, that you can make this work, make it something people care about, then go for it. *You* know best.

What is your favorite thing about your workspace?

I have a few: our swing, confetti drawer, and prop box, which holds lots of silly things such as hats and boas. Sometimes you just need to wear a Viking hat to respond to a difficult e-mail. I believe that you do your best work when you're having fun.

Name a fear or professional challenge that keeps you up at night.

Keeping up with e-mail. It's my primary source of guilt.

Name the biggest overall lesson you've learned in running a business.

A company is a living, breathing organism. It can adapt to any challenge as long as I lead from the heart and my team feels appreciated and heard.

What quotation or saying inspires and motivates you to be yourself and do what you love?

"Success is liking yourself, liking what you do, and liking how you do it." —Maya Angelou

At what point in your life did you first learn about your field of work? What called you to it?

When I was about seven, on vacation in the South of France, I watched my uncle draw type. I asked him, "What are you doing?" And he said, "I am working!" I was confused, as in my understanding, he was just doodling, drawing, having fun. So I followed up, saying, "Working, as in making money?" And he just said, "Yep!" I was a kid who was never not drawing. It was as if a lightbulb went off in my head. "I can make money off drawing type? Drawing can be my profession?" This makes me understand how important it is to expose my kids to as many different "worlds" as possible.

Name your greatest success (or something you're most proud of) in your business experiences.

I am probably most proud of the fact that the simple idea of CreativeMornings, hosting an accessible, free event for my creative community, has resonated with so many people around the world that we are now a global organization of over a thousand volunteers putting on events monthly. For free. And we are growing by three to five chapters a month. What started in my studio has become a global labor of love. CreativeMornings has shown me that when you put trust in people, they will overdeliver and surprise you. Trust is the biggest compliment of all. Trust breeds magic.

WITH DEEP RESPECT TO DOYALD YOUNG

In your opinion, what are the top three things someone should consider before starting a business?

I have one: Don't start a business unless the idea keeps you up at night because you're *so excited* about it. You need that fire in you to get past the hurdles that you will encounter.

Knowing what you know now, what would you have done differently when you were first starting out?

I would have started my own company sooner. I started my design studio the day my daughter was born. She was basically my biggest career catalyst. I thought I wasn't ready before that. I was waiting for that angelic choir to come down from heaven to tell me I should start my business *now*. But what I realized is that perfect moment doesn't exist. The perfect moment is when you realize you actually want to start your own business and you have the freedom to make it happen. Take small steps but work your way toward it. Don't wait. Also, your twenties are the ideal time to experiment.

Which of your traits are you most proud of?

I can raise enthusiasm around an idea and get people excited. If I were a superhero, I would be Captain Enthusiasm.

What is your personal or professional motto?

"The best way to complain is to make things." —James Murphy

What's your favorite thing to come home to after a long day of work?

The hugs of my kids.

"Success means being able to generate projects actively, rather than passively waiting for things to fall into my lap."

Ayumi Horie

Potter
Portland, ME

What did you want to be when you were a child?

I wanted to be an archaeologist. I loved the idea of working in dirt and discovering new things, though as it turned out, I still get to do those things as a potter.

Name a fear or professional challenge that keeps you up at night.

I worry about sustainability and how to shift my business model as I grow older. Making pots is physically demanding, and I want to be able to continue as a maker without either wrecking my body or passing off important tasks to others. Part of the strength of my work is that each and every piece is the result of more than a dozen creative decisions. The challenge I face is how to keep the handmade charm and quirkiness of each piece, while making them more accessible to a wider audience.

What is your favorite thing about your workspace?

My favorite thing about my studio is that I can sit in a nook yet be in a high-ceilinged, open space. It allows me to feel cozy while looking out at the bigger picture, whether it's a broad worktable, the snow piling up outside, or the schedule for the rest of the week.

What does success mean to you?

Success means being able to generate projects actively, rather than passively waiting for things to fall into my lap. In some ways, my bread-and-butter ceramic work subsidizes other projects that may not make income, yet are creatively meaningful.

Name the biggest overall lesson you've learned in running a business.

The lesson I've learned over and over is not to compromise on quality. Even though it might take twice as long to attend to all the tiny details necessary to make something shipshape, it's worth the effort.

Name your greatest success (or something you're most proud of) in your business experiences.

Handmade For Japan, which was a fund-raiser I cofounded that raised over $100,000 for disaster relief in Japan after the Great East Japan Earthquake and Tsunami. In the way I do business, there's not much boundary between my personal and work life. I think businesses *ought* to take on projects that come from the heart and benefit the community, even if they're expensive in a traditional business model. I don't think I had a choice about cofounding Handmade For Japan, because every bone in my body felt like it was the right thing to do.

What tool, object, or ritual could you not live without in your workday?

My iPhone. I wish I could say it was something healthy like meditation or cold-pressed kale juice, but those things just make me shrug. (I know I'll regret it!) My phone is the tool, the object, and the ritual. I'm not always in the ceramics studio, but I'm always working, always researching and looking at work, mostly on Instagram. The work I do with @potsinaction and social media is as much a part of me now as my pots are.

What's the first thing you do every morning to start your day on the right foot?

I choose a coffee cup. We have countless cups from different potters and potter-friends. The choice is very intuitive and revealing. The decision about which cup to use is a mix of which potter-friend I want to be reminded of, aesthetics, and practical things like volume, shape, and material. Setting off the day with a reminder of a friendship and a connection through an object is a great way to make it a good day.

I talk to friends who are level and supportive and then I put my head down and get back to work. Working hard makes me remember what my core values are, and through the making, I remember the things I love.

> "I'm really not very good at bullshit. If I'm saying something, I believe it. It's fun to come into grown womanhood, being direct and forthright."

Melissa Harris-Perry

Professor, Journalist
Winston-Salem, NC

What did you want to be when you were a child?

At one point I wanted to be an archaeologist, and then I found out how painstaking and patient one must be in that process, and that's not my personality. I'm a little more "rush in." In high school I wanted to be a children's psychiatrist and help kids, but halfway through college I think I'd figured out I wanted to be a teacher of some kind. Once the professor path became clear to me, there's never been anything else I've wanted to be.

What was the best piece of business advice you were given when you were starting out?

The best piece of advice I was given was actually related to pregnancy. Someone told me, "The days will be long, but the years will be short."

What is your favorite thing about your workspace?

I've been waiting for this workspace for a long time. This is my dream house, my forever house. I knew the moment I walked in that this was home. I love the light coming in across the front porch. But mostly I love that my office is connected to our family room and across from my husband—I feel like I can see what's going on and talk to everyone at all times.

Name a fear or professional challenge that keeps you up at night.

At all points I'm always afraid that my tendency to just say whatever it is I think, in an unfiltered way, will have negative consequences on my family and my team.

Has learning from a mistake ever led you to success?

That's my *whole* story. I followed a boy to college. Which is a terrible, terrible reason to go to a college. But looking back I find I often make the right decision for the wrong reasons. I picked this college (Wake Forest) in part because my high school boyfriend was going to college right up the road at Chapel Hill. But this was very much the right decision and the right school for me.

In moments of self-doubt or adversity, how do you build yourself back up?

I am not capable of building myself back up. I need other people's help to do that for or with me. It's really about turning to the lovely people in my life who unconditionally love me. That includes my family, my husband, and even my staff and team members at work. We've had some hard times at the show and I've had producers who will back me up and say, "Let's do this." So feeling that is powerful and helpful.

Name your greatest success (or something you're most proud of) in your business experiences.

I really like my second book, *Sister Citizen*. Every time I meet someone at a lecture or in class and they have a copy of it dog-eared or quote it back to me, it means the world to me. I worked on that book for a ridiculously long time, and I'm quite proud of it.

What does the world need more of? Less of?

My world needs more time to read. I wish we had more space for engaging with the written word. Everybody's schedule has gotten so busy that it's hard to find the time to sit and read. We could legitimately use a little bit less presumption that we know all the answers, and a little more curiosity. It's great to crawl up a new learning curve.

Which of your traits are you most proud of?

It's probably the same one that keeps me up at night. I'm really not very good at bullshit. If I'm saying something, I believe it. It's fun to come into grown womanhood, being direct and forthright.

If you were magically given three more hours per day, what would you do with them?

Write. I would write. That's literally what I need. Three hours a day—in six months my next book would be done. Is that an offer? Do you have them with you?

Those are moments when I feel like I'm contributing something but I'm also receiving something. Reciprocity feels like success.

"You can't win if you don't play."

Kristina Gill

Development Adviser, Food Editor/ Photographer
Rome, Italy

What did you want to be when you were a child?

I don't remember, actually, but at some point I am sure I wanted to be president of the United States.

What characteristic do you most admire in other creative women?

The ability to stay truly unique.

What does success mean to you?

That's really a question I've been grappling with for quite a while. In photography, I suppose for me success is producing an image that moves someone, that remains in someone's head. In food editing, I think it is someone choosing a recipe you've shared and making it their own. As a development adviser, it is getting the right information at the right time to get a contribution that will save lives. In life, I think it changes as I change and encounter different challenges. Lately, being able to provide and care for my family has been my measure of success.

What is the biggest sacrifice you've made in your career/line of work?

There are two—moving back to the United States, and having a child. With the move back, it is a double-edged sword because I think I have had more professional opportunities here than I would have had on the same trajectory in the United States, but I miss having seen my family regularly and having seen my nieces and nephews grow up. With having a child, I kept thinking, Right after I reach this goal, I can finally take some time off.

In moments of self-doubt or adversity, how do you build yourself back up?

I discovered a few years ago that whenever I am feeling at my worst, I research a few photo editors and dream publications/contacts, and I pitch or reach out. I have had a pretty good response rate to date, and that reaffirms, through objective eyes, the value of my work. I also look at others' portfolios and listen to the *Entrepreneurs* podcast by Monocle, which always gets me thinking about new projects.

What quotation or saying inspires and motivates you to be yourself and do what you love?

Seems simple, but it always comes back to "You can't win if you don't play."

Which of your traits are you most proud of?

My perseverance in the face of adversity.

What would you tell yourself ten to twenty years ago that you wish you knew then?

Three things: (1) Don't be cheap when it comes to investing in yourself and your goals. If you aren't willing to invest in yourself, why should anyone else? (2) Never let what other people (including parents) might think influence your choices. (3) In difficult situations where you are panicking about a mistake, just ask yourself, "Will this matter in five years?" (The answer is almost always no.)

Name a woman (or women), past or present, whom you admire or look up to.

I admire women who overcome extreme obstacles to pursue the profession/career/activity they love or the cause they believe in.

"Creativity comes naturally to me, but the business side was something I had to teach myself."

Diana Yen

Food Stylist, Author
New York, NY

What did you want to be when you were a child?

I wanted to be an architect at a very young age. I loved spending hours drawing and dreaming up homes for my hamsters to live in. I've always loved making things. As I got older I became more social and happier making things that could be shared with others.

What was the best piece of business advice you were given when you were starting out?

When you start a creative business, it's easy to get wrapped up in your vision for things. Someone told me that if I wanted to make it in New York City, I couldn't only think like an artist. I would have to learn to recognize business opportunities and the needs of my clients. Creativity comes naturally to me, but the business side was something I had to teach myself.

What is your favorite thing about your workspace?

I live in Brooklyn Heights, and it's always inspiring for me to come to the Lower East Side to my studio every day. I thrive on the ever-changing energy of the city. I also love having Cleo, my Angora bunny, hang out with me under my desk.

Name a fear or professional challenge that keeps you up at night.

Deciding how much staffing to have can be difficult for a small studio. If you don't have enough help, you'll stunt business growth, and if you have too much, your overhead becomes too high during slow times. There was a time that we did large-scale catering and I had more staff, but I realized I wasn't happy managing other people. It paid well, but I'd rather be deep in the creative process. So I decided to cut down on that side of the business and only do the jobs I want to do. I hire freelancers when it's necessary.

What quotation or saying inspires and motivates you to be yourself and do what you love?

"It seems to me that our three basic needs, for food and security and love, are so mixed and mingled and entwined that we cannot straightly think of one without the others. So it happens that when I write of hunger, I am really writing about love and the hunger for it, and warmth and the love of it and the hunger for it . . . and then the warmth and richness and fine reality of hunger satisfied . . . and it is all one." —M. F. K. Fisher

Knowing what you know now, what would you have done differently when you were first starting out?

I started my business in my late twenties and took the plunge without much financial planning. I poured all my resources into growing and maintaining my business, without much thought. I just wanted to focus on the fun and dreamy things. Now that I'm in my thirties, I'm seeing that my overhead is incredibly high with two rents (studio and home). Rent is basically your money going into a black hole. I wish that I had bought an apartment when I had the cushy job before I started my business. The more financial stability you can lock in earlier, the more you have a nice foundation to build your business on.

Where were you when you came up with the idea for your business or discovered what you wanted to do?

I was at the Martha Stewart craft show selling cookies with my friend, and the editors wanted us to demo them on TV. I was thrilled! They asked if we had a business and I lied and said yes so we could get on the show. In two weeks, we designed a website, got a business license, and connected with a bakery to produce the cookies. I'm very focused on seasonal cooking and discovering the hidden treasures in New York City, so I decided to call my business the Jewels of New York.

What is your no-fail go-to when you need inspiration or to get out of a creative rut?

I travel somewhere that has a strong culinary tradition to get inspired. My ideal situation is to rent an apartment and go to food markets all day. Then I come home and do some freestyle cooking with all the amazing produce.

> "I haven't had to make any sacrifices for my work. Those were made in the past when I *wasn't* doing what I do now."

Jennie Jieun Lee

Ceramicist
Brooklyn, NY

What did you want to be when you were a child?
A visual artist like my mother.

What was the best piece of business advice you were given when you were starting out?
I was working as a casting agent for my friend Anita Bitton when she told me it's important to *be consistent*. I take that into consideration every week.

What is your favorite thing about your workspace?
My privacy and the natural sunlight. But when I open the door, I have access to my friends who do woodworking and metal work.

Name the biggest overall lesson you've learned in running a business.
It's okay not to know everything all the time.

What is the biggest sacrifice you've made in starting or running your business?

I haven't had to make any sacrifices for my work. Those were made in the past when I *wasn't* doing what I do now.

In moments of self-doubt or adversity, how do you build yourself back up?

I watch videos and read interviews with other artists. The window into other creatives' worlds always helps because self-doubt is so common.

What quotation or saying inspires and motivates you to be yourself and do what you love?

"I'm not for everybody."

At what point in your life did you first learn about your field of work? What called you to it?

My mother was an art teacher in Korea, so I grew up making things and seeing the world through her painting/printmaking filter from early on.

What resources would you recommend to someone starting a creative business?

Take what you love and study every aspect of it. Watch movies, read books and magazines, listen to podcasts, travel to study it, and talk to others doing the same work.

What does the world need more of? Less of?

More *hygge*. Fewer people.

What tool, object, or ritual could you not live without in your workday?

Water.

What is your personal or professional motto?

It takes a lot of work to be this normal.

"I'm proud of the fact that I'm always making things."

Carson Ellis

Artist, Illustrator
Tualatin, OR

What did you want to be when you were a child?

I wanted to be an artist or a naturalist.

What characteristic do you most admire in other creative women?

I admire women who are funny and women who are gross. I admire smart, obsessive women who are managing to reference a lifetime of accumulated knowledge in their art while simultaneously forgetting everything they know to make art mystically, with abandon. I admire men who do that too.

What is your favorite thing about your workspace?

I like that it's pretty bright and that it's in the middle of a field. It has double doors that open up in the summer and a woodstove that keeps it cozy through the gloomy Oregon winter. I like that I have to pass by my big vegetable garden on the way to and from it every day, which reminds me that there's a world outside to be tended to, not only the often all-consuming inner world of my own imagination and illustration practice.

Which of your traits are you most proud of?

I'm proud of the fact that I'm always making things. I would draw, paint, knit, sew, garden, and build even if there was no one to do it for.

What does the world need more of? Less of?

More food for hungry kids, money for teachers and librarians, grants for higher education, paid maternity and paternity leave, livable wages for workers, neurodiversity enlightenment, and horror movies that don't suck. Less police brutality and automatic weapons.

What would you tell yourself ten to twenty years ago that you wish you knew then?

I would tell myself to be more autonomous as an illustrator; to trust my instincts and not give in to bad design decisions to avoid seeming difficult. But I'd also remind myself not to be unduly difficult, because I often was back then. I'd tell myself that it's possible to stick steadfastly by your vision without being a jerk.

Name a woman (or women), past or present, whom you admire or look up to.

I admire the children's book editor Ursula Nordstrom. She edited just about every brave and formative kids' book you can think of from the '40s through the '70s, a period of creative revolution in children's literature that she spearheaded. We have her to thank for books like *Where the Wild Things Are*, *Goodnight Moon*, *Harriet the Spy*, *Charlotte's Web*, and *The Giving Tree*—not because she wrote them but because they were weird books that simply wouldn't have been published without an influential and headstrong champion. She was a powerful gay woman in midcentury America. (She became Harper's first female senior vice president in 1960.) And she was hilarious and brilliant. Her motto was "Good books for bad children."

> "Having patience means being at peace with the time it takes to do something right and to its fullest."

Jonna Twigg

Bookbinder
Brooklyn, NY

What did you want to be when you were a child?
I wanted to be an architect or engineer. I wanted to build and design really unique buildings with cool materials. My bubble burst when I understood how much advanced mathematics was involved.

What was the best piece of business advice you were given when you were starting out?
I was told to always trust in my vision and to not be afraid of risk taking. I find that as you open yourself up to the public you're also inviting numerous opinions into your head space. It's important to know yourself and to remain focused on what you've set out to do, while always being ready to seize an opportunity.

What is your favorite thing about your workspace?
I really love the material bank I built. This enormous piece of furniture makes our materials and processes visible to customers while also keeping us organized. Seeing everything laid out just the way I envisioned is a delight each morning when I open the doors. I also see the ways in which people are inspired when they're able to see the components of a project. I think it allows them to visualize themselves making something by hand, which is always positive.

Name the biggest overall lesson you've learned in running a business.
Patience—with myself first and foremost. It's a lesson I seem to relearn every year. I find it's so important to understand timing and to be strategic in my various projects. Having patience means being at peace with the time it takes to do something right and to its fullest.

Name your greatest success (or something you're most proud of) in your business experiences.
Personally my biggest success is the way in which I've transformed myself. It's no small feat to go from a person who identifies primarily as an artist to one who calls herself a business owner/entrepreneur/manager. It requires constant education and the confidence to wear those titles in the world. It's been so rewarding to realize how creative you get to be in business as well.

What tool, object, or ritual could you not live without in your workday?
I have too many essential tools to name just one. However, the ritual of cleaning my workspace at the end of the day and Knolling my tools [the process of arranging like objects in parallel or 90-degree angles as a method of organization] is so satisfying. It allows my brain to feel at peace with the day's work, and then in the morning I'm off to a better start.

Name a woman (or women), past or present, whom you admire or look up to.
My mother is an enormous inspiration to me. Her demonstration of hard work, business savvy, and creative problem solving—all while remaining serenely calm and encouraging to my brother, sister, and me—is something I marvel at all the time. I hope to mature into that woman and become such an example for my family someday as well.

"I've always found the power to regain my strength or confidence in the pages of books."

Ashley C. Ford

Writer
Brooklyn, NY

What did you want to be when you were a child?

As a child, I couldn't think of anything I wanted to be more than an actor. My grandmother loved movies, and for a time, we saw one together every Saturday. She'd pick one, then I'd pick one, then she'd pick one, and so on. I often chose mine based on the poster outside the theater. All the most fabulous black women I saw were in movies, or on my television. That was my measure of success. Would I be Angela Bassett or Oprah? I didn't stop thinking I'd be an actor until I was seventeen. Now I know my true desire has always been to be a storyteller more than anything else, and there are many ways to be a storyteller. However, to be honest, I often still miss the stage.

What was the best piece of business advice you were given when you were starting out?

That your first step is just that: the first of many steps. For so long I would stand still, afraid to move in any direction because I wasn't sure which was the course I wanted to follow for the rest of my life. Finally, someone explained to me that my first steps did not necessarily determine one path for all my tomorrows. There would be more decisions, and more opportunities to make a shift should I need to do so. Nothing has ever made me feel less afraid to simply try something new. It was an assurance of freedom I desperately needed.

What is your favorite thing about your workspace?

My workspace is inundated with books. They're above me, beside me, and right in front of me. I did not grow up owning many books because we couldn't afford them. All my books came from the library or school, or I won them in reading contests and reading programs. Now I live a life where people send me books for free, my partner works in a bookstore, and if I really want a book, I can usually afford to buy it. For me, my books represent the realization of a big part of my dream life.

What is the biggest sacrifice you've made in starting or running your business?

In my family, nothing was coveted more than financial stability. The epitome of success was knowing you had money showing up regularly, and that money would cover all your expenses. It's a dream a lot of families have. In choosing to work for myself, I've given up access to that kind of stability for the time being. I decided that the chance to build something of my own, especially while I don't have children or a mortgage, was an opportunity I couldn't pass up. Right now, it's a hustle. But it's my hustle.

What does success mean to you?

Success to me is always having options. It's one thing to decide you don't want to have something, do something, or go somewhere, but it's quite another to know you can't.

Name a fear or professional challenge that keeps you up at night.

I'm still terrible at asking for help. Don't get me wrong—I have been helped. Most of the success of my life can be attributed to those who forced their help on me. My friend and mentor, Roxane Gay [page 85], doesn't even really ask to help me anymore. She just does it, and refuses to let me give her crap about it. I have good people in my life, and I try to be good to them. There's nothing wrong with allowing them to be good to me too.

Name the biggest overall lesson you've learned in running a business.
Keep. Records. Of. Everything.

Has learning from a mistake ever led you to success?
I once agreed to write about something deeply personal, something I'd never written or even talked about much before, and after working on it for a week decided I couldn't write it. Instead of telling my editor, I just sort of hid. It was one of the first freelance assignments I'd ever taken on, and I was terrified that she would hate me. We'd never even met! After a while, I answered her e-mail and let her know what had happened. She told me that the subject matter was sensitive, and she understood, but radio silence wasn't exactly helpful. From then on, I realized that it was okay to find yourself behind, but don't let your anxiety stop you from sending that little e-mail that tells your editor what's going on.

In moments of self-doubt or adversity, how do you build yourself back up?
I read. I've always found the power to regain my strength or confidence in the pages of books. That could mean rereading a favorite book, or finding a new one to fall in love with. Either way, books have always been a solid foundation for me, sturdy ground. If I can find my way there, I can get through anything. I feel buoyed, protected, and understood. Books have saved me more than once. Indeed, they save me over and over again.

What quotation or saying inspires and motivates you to be yourself and do what you love?
"There is no greater agony than bearing an untold story inside you." —Maya Angelou

Knowing what you know now, what would you have done differently when you were first starting out?
I would have saved more money. A lot more money.

What does the world need more of? Less of?
The world needs more empathy, and less addiction to certainty.

Which of your traits are you most proud of?

I am always trying to be a better person than I was the day before.

What is your no-fail go-to when you need inspiration or to get out of a creative rut?
I reread the book *Walk Two Moons* by Sharon Creech. It's a middle-grade book about the bravest child I've ever "known," and her name is Salamanca Tree Hiddle. She is my muse, and all the best things about me are learned from her.

What's the first thing you do every morning to start your day on the right foot?
If I have bacon and fruit, it's going to be a good day.

Name a woman (or women), past or present, whom you admire or look up to.
There are so many. Dr. Maya Angelou, Sally Mann, Toni Morrison, Grace Jones, Roxane Gay, Oprah, Eartha Kitt, Harriet Tubman, Shonda Rhimes, Elizabeth Gilbert, and that's just to name a few. I am inspired by so many women.

What is your personal or professional motto?

You are more than the worst thing you've ever done.

"Jumping in and being a little uncomfortable is part of the process of growing my business."

Jessica Marquez

Artist, Crafter
Brooklyn, NY

What did you want to be when you were a child?
Always an artist, but I also considered being the person at the top of the ski lift who takes your family's portrait. I wanted to be outdoors and ski all the time. That seemed like the next best option to a ten-year-old obsessed with neon ski suits and flying downhill.

What was the best piece of business advice you were given when you were starting out?
I had a lot of supportive friends and family telling me to just start. I was so full of doubt that I had a hard time hearing them. I thought I had to have everything figured out beforehand. I definitely still don't, but now I know that jumping in and being a little uncomfortable is just part of the process of growing my business.

What's the first thing you do every morning to start your day on the right foot?
My alarm goes off every morning with the phrase, "Make it the best day." It's a good reminder for me that I have a choice in the matter. I'd much rather sleep in, but somehow seeing that phrase motivates me to get going.

Name the biggest overall lesson you've learned in running a business.

Put yourself out there. I never thought I'd write a book, share my work online, or see my handmade products in shops, but the more I built up momentum, the easier it was to reach out and make opportunities happen.

What is your favorite thing about your workspace?

I really have a love-hate relationship with my chaotic, jam-packed studio space/second bedroom/that room where you hide stuff when you have company. It's messy and unorganized, but it's my space. I love that I can be in there with no judgments at all hours of the night with a cat by my side or underfoot making a mess.

What does success mean to you?

To be thriving! To be working with people, stores, and other businesses I admire. I've said yes to projects in the past that might not have been the right fit, but I wanted to get my foot in the door. Being able to have more control and still have steady work would mean I'm growing in the right direction.

Has learning from a mistake ever led you to success?

I stopped working for a while. I felt lost and heartbroken when my father passed away a few years ago, and I just didn't want to work alone anymore. So I started to do more photography and set Miniature Rhino aside for a bit. Stepping away hurt. Looking back, it wasn't a mistake, although it truly felt like it was at the time, because it turned into an opportunity to diversify my work and gave me time to refresh. When I was ready, I came back more passionate and excited than ever.

What resources would you recommend to someone starting a creative business?

Get to know your camera and how to use it well, even if it's just the camera on your phone. You need beautiful imagery to help your business grow, whether you're providing a service or a physical product you're making. Being my own photographer has been a powerful tool and resource for me.

In your opinion, what are the top three things someone should consider before starting a business?

I wish someone had sat me down and asked me about my products. "Can you make a lot of these? Can you scale production? Can your prices support wholesale?" No, no, and no. I didn't know that I should be thinking about these specific things and was undervaluing my work. I started out making hand embroidery, which is very time-consuming. It could have succeeded if I changed my pricing and how I worked, but what was better for me was creating kits from my designs, teaching, and writing a book about it.

What is your no-fail go-to when you need inspiration or to get out of a creative rut?

I'll pull a bunch of books off the shelf and thumb through them, mostly old books and illustrated children's books. Children's books are my favorite—the illustrations, stories, and colors always seem to inspire me and bring me a lot of pleasure to just sit and enjoy.

Name a woman (or women), past or present, whom you admire or look up to.

In the creative business world I admire Natalie Chanin [page 330] of Alabama Chanin. Her books and clothes are beautiful and inspiring, but also the business itself is an inspiration—an embroidered fashion line made locally and all by hand. In creative life I greatly admire Louise Bourgeois. Totally fearless, open, and never stopped making.

If you were magically given three more hours per day, what would you do with them?

Go outside more, taking long, directionless walks, and read more.

"It takes ten years to become an overnight success."

Anishka Clarke

Interior Designer
Brooklyn, NY

What did you want to be when you were a child?

First and foremost I needed to be a ballerina. This was definitely my first career choice. At one point, at the age of ten or so, I remember wanting to write children's books. And I did. Prior to that, though, I think my burning desire was always fashion design. My mom sewed a lot and so I became fascinated with it. I learned to operate the machine, I hand sewed, cut and sewed McCall patterns and doll clothes, and even made bags and sold them in high school. I also went to embroidery class for a while. Not sure when or even if this has waned, as I do have somewhere at the bottom of my future goals list "clothing line."

What was the best piece of business advice you were given when you were starting out?

One of my professors encouraged me to work for a few designers of differing styles before going out on my own, in an effort to broaden my design aesthetic and get really good at many. Unfortunately, I was too set on starting Ishka Designs to heed the advice. Fortunately for us, our clients' tastes seem to run the spectrum of styles and as such we think our portfolio of work over the last few years shows a healthy depth of diversity. Ultimately, what he wanted me to gain through apprenticeship, I learned through a "deliver no matter what" attitude.

Has learning from a mistake ever led you to success?

One of the first and best lessons we learned very early on was how to manage expectations. We had quite the fiasco of a project in our first year, and since then we are very careful of how we manage expectations, always emphasizing both the best- and worst-case scenarios from the jump.

What quotation or saying inspires and motivates you to be yourself and do what you love?

"It takes ten years to become an overnight success."

At what point in your life did you first learn about your field of work? What called you to it?

I was a year or two into owning my first apartment and somewhat unhappy in my finance career. My choice of decor and innovative wall solution led friends to my door, wanting me to assist with their own. One late November, while in the process of decorating one such friend's home, I had a call with a jeweler friend. She was lamenting the fact that her assistant was leaving for a better-paying job with perks, etc., because her husband was going back to school to study architecture. He was doing what? At age thirty? *Ding ding ding*! The next day I picked two New York City–based schools and submitted my applications a few days later. The rest is history.

What does the world need more of? Less of?

We need more positive media, news, and people. We need more diversity. We need more hugs. We need more support systems.

We need less mindless reality TV. We need less negative news. We need less ignorance, less homogenous thinking, and fewer judgments.

Name a woman (or women), past or present, whom you admire or look up to.

Oprah. Nina Simone. My mom.

"When I was a child, I wanted to be a bird, or a flying horse or something wild."

Carmen Argote

Artist
Los Angeles, CA

What did you want to be when you were a child?

When I was a child, I wanted to be a bird, or a flying horse or something wild. Later on, when I realized that the question was about a profession, I think I always thought I would go into the sciences. I had no idea you could be an artist.

What is your favorite thing about your workspace?

My favorite thing about my workspace is that I live in it and experience it constantly through habit.

Name the biggest overall lesson you've learned in running a business.

I think it's very important to know what you are good at and what you need help with, and to surround yourself with people who will and want to contribute to your success. I have also learned that the best policy is to compensate people for their work with a fair wage.

Has learning from a mistake ever led you to success?

I have made many mistakes. I think the mistake I made for the longest time in terms of my art practice was to devalue my own experiences. I remember researching what to make artwork about and not drawing from my personal history.

In learning from this mistake, I have emerged a better artist who can think of her practice long term. I look at everything I have as a resource, and now I am able to continually find inspiration and express myself with an artistic voice that feels authentic to who I am.

Name your greatest success (or something you're most proud of) in your business experiences.

I feel very proud of my exhibition *720 Sq. Ft.: Household Mutations* that I did in 2010. It was entirely self-funded and I used the carpeting from my childhood home to talk about architecture in a very personal way. It was the first time I worked outside of an institution, wrote a proposal, created a budget, and approached the ideal space, gallery G727, with my proposal. This exhibition really taught me how to pave my own path and work both within and outside of institutional support.

What does the world need more of? Less of?

I believe the world needs more of an awareness of our interconnectedness and less of a focus on the idea of the individual.

What is your no-fail go-to when you need inspiration or to get out of a creative rut?

I start by walking around the neighborhood I grew up in, Pico Union in Los Angeles. I look at everything that is still there and all the things that have changed. I look at how people use the city streets, and how people invent new ways of doing things.

Name a woman (or women), past or present, whom you admire or look up to.

There are many women whom I admire, starting with my mother. There are also many artists and curators who have inspired, motivated, and challenged me. I am grateful to writers, especially Toni Morrison—her novels and writings have been particularly moving to me. Her writing seems to stem from something so intimate and personal and expands into everything else. It changes everything around me—how I see and what I know. I admire her immensely.

> "Fear does not keep me up at night. Sometimes I'll stay up for prayer. Or dancing. But never for fear. I'm too exhausted for fear."

Matika Wilbur

Photographer
Seattle, WA

What did you want to be when you were a child?

I wanted to be a professional basketball player, even though the Women's Basketball Association didn't exist yet. I guess I innately believed in women's liberation before I understood the concept of feminism. By the time I was in high school, I'd accepted that I would never be a professional ballplayer (I blame my coordination), and since I had passion and skill in the visual arts, I decided to work toward that identity and lifestyle instead.

What was the best piece of business advice you were given when you were starting out?

When I was sixteen, I earned a place in the summer intensive program at the Rocky Mountain School of Photography. When I received the letter of acceptance, I shook with glee until I realized that I would need $7,000 to attend. I told my mom, Nancy, a determined, successful deep-sea fisherwoman with several other thriving businesses, that I couldn't go because we couldn't afford it. I would just stay home to tend the family fishing business. She said, "Matika,

let's stop thinking about the reasons you can't go, and let's focus on what will be required to make it happen." We came up with the money and that was my first lesson in "getting it done": Step 1: Figure out what is required. Step 2: Make it happen.

What is your favorite thing about your workspace?

I currently live and work out of a 2005 Volkswagen Rialta RV, traveling the country taking photographs of more than 562 federally recognized Native American tribes in the United States for a photo- and narrative-based documentary, *Project 562* (though it's morphed creatively into much more than pictures and stories). My favorite thing about my cozy rolling workspace, aka "the Big Girl," is that she gets incredible gas mileage, and she can hang with me anywhere, bringing along all my equipment, clothes, personal belongings, bed, food, and, yup, a bathroom.

What is the biggest sacrifice you've made in starting or running your business?

I remember reading somewhere (or maybe everywhere) that we can have it all—success in our careers, the rom-com love life, the *Leave It To Beaver* family, and a fabulous apartment with a view. But I haven't gotten to those things quite yet. I get to do what I love every day in a life full of constant adventure while connecting with people, making photographs, and taking in stories about things that I believe matter while eating really good food, breathing, doing yoga, sleeping occasionally, and sometimes (rarely) going on a hot date. But I haven't made the money yet, or found a partner, and I live in the Big Girl, which really can't touch a nice apartment. Following my passion has cost me much of what I envision as part of the "good" life. But I'd never change it; I've gained too much.

What does success mean to you?

I am from the Swinomish and Tulalip tribes of Washington State, which means I come from "the people of the tide" and the "salmon people." Historically, the noblest thing one could do in our community is host a potlatch, where we would invite relatives and friends from surrounding communities and feed them. Songs

327

and prayers would be shared, babies would get their "Indian" names, lovers would be married, our deceased would be honored, and so on. At the end of the potlatch, the host family would give all of their possessions away to the attendees—precious baskets, food stores, and canoes; they'd essentially impoverish themselves. It was honorable to love your people so much that you would give them everything you have. And to me, that is the type of success that I strive for.

Name a fear or professional challenge that keeps you up at night.
Fear does not keep me up at night. Sometimes I'll stay up for prayer. Or dancing. But never for fear. I'm too exhausted for fear.

What quotation or saying inspires you and motivates you to be yourself and do what you love?

"We don't live like nobody's watching. We live like our ancestors are watching."

If you were given $100 million, would you run your business any differently? How so?
Yes, I'd hire "superpeople." We'd work in education, media, and music, and I'd create a fun, get-things-done professional and business network, like a consortium to celebrate Native artistic and intellectual talent. (There's so much out there!) And I'd support important battles and challenges that my people, especially Native children and women, are up against.

What is your personal or professional motto?
To treat each new encounter with the love and warmth that I offer old friends.

In moments of self-doubt or adversity, how do you build yourself back up?
I pray.

Name your greatest success (or something you're most proud of) in your business experiences.
I recently met a young Native woman who traveled for hours with her dad to attend my presentation and workshops. She confided that she had been struggling with addiction and suicidal impulses until she discovered my work, and that it inspired her to turn her life around. These kinds of encounters can't help but make me feel what I'm doing has worth.

In your opinion, what are the top three things someone should consider before starting a business?
1. What are your intentions? Are they aligned with your spirit?
2. Are you really in love with the business (because you should be) or is it just lust, especially for money?
3. Are you doing it to be of service in some way? Business is difficult; it requires a lot of strength and courage. If you know you can add to the world through what you want to do, then you'll find inside what you need to make it happen.

What does the world need more of? Less of?
More love, tolerance, and peace. Less hatred and power.

Business is like a fruit tree. There are several life cycles before the bearing stage; and even though we know that it will take several generations to bear fruit, we plant it anyway because our grandchildren will relish what we produced or created for them.

> "Examine your life and how you want to exist. That way, you can design your business around those things, and you will know when you get there."

Natalie Chanin

Fashion Designer
Florence, AL

What did you want to be when you were a child?

I dreamed of becoming a zoologist/journalist/photographer who specialized in dolphins and other magical creatures of land and sea.

What was the best piece of business advice you were given when you were starting out?

A good friend (who also happens to be my lawyer) told me early on to "determine how much is enough for you" from the beginning. What he meant was to examine your life and how you want to exist. That way, you can design your business around those things, and you will know when you get there. Being satisfied has a lot to do with knowing your own desires.

What is your favorite thing about your workspace?

My workspace is ever-changing but feels permanent. Everything is on wheels and moves pretty regularly. I think it is important to have these designated workspaces—but to also break them up and move them when a project or stage calls for a different construction.

Name a fear or professional challenge that keeps you up at night.

Cash flow. Cash flow. Cash flow. It is a good thing that many businesses are started by the young because older, more financially savvy people might never make the leap. I always advise those who want to start their own businesses to learn as much as possible about accounting, saving, and investing. Many families count on me and on the business I created to put food on their tables. That is not a responsibility I take lightly.

Has learning from a mistake ever led you to success?

The closing of the first iteration of my company felt like the end of the world at the time. But it turned out to be the beginning of a new sort of company that allowed us to use mistakes from the first go-round to create (or strive to create) a more sustainable model that is, in reality, much closer to the company that we wanted in the beginning anyway.

In moments of self-doubt or adversity, how do you build yourself back up?

I'm very grounded in my community and my family. I've learned sometimes to walk away and take a break when self-doubt appears. Sometimes dinner with your family, a bit of gardening, and a good night's sleep make everything seem possible again. Go back in the morning and turn to your team—they almost always know the answer anyway.

> "I admire women who are open and vulnerable about the self-doubt that happens in the creative process and yet go forward and do it anyway."

Aarti Sequeira

Chef, Television Host
Los Angeles, CA

What did you want to be when you were a child?

Well, apart from a superhero, I think I did want to be a cooking show host. But I blacked that out of my memory, and I only remembered it when I was older and I was talking to a friend of mine and I was like, "You know when you were little and you played cooking show host?" And she looked at me with this blank stare, and then she goes, "No, Aarti, not everyone played cooking show host."

What characteristic do you most admire in other creative women?

I used to say I admired women who never doubted themselves, who have no fear and could just kind of roar it out and do it. But I've changed my mind, because I actually don't think that exists. I admire women who are open and vulnerable about the self-doubt that happens in the creative process and yet go forward and do it anyway.

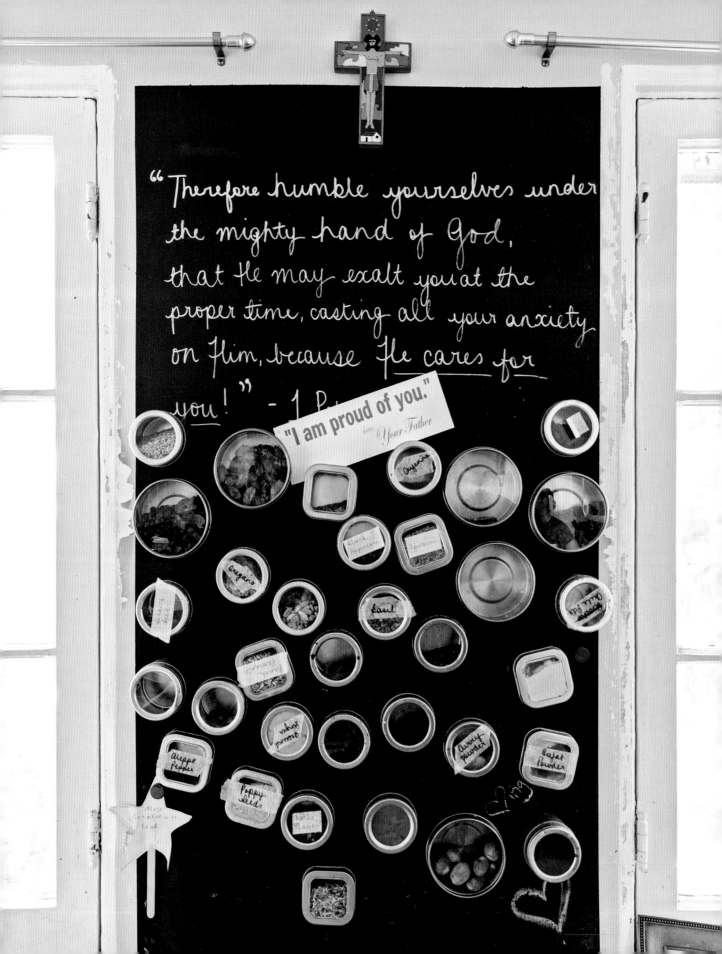

What does success mean to you?

There are two parts of me. There's the over-achiever side of me: culturally, I was brought up to achieve, achieve, achieve, because by achieving, you bring the next generation along with you. The other definition of success is when something I do or say is helpful to someone else. Just the other day, on my Facebook page, I received four messages from women who had watched me compete on a Food Network show, where I was playing for an organization called Postpartum Support International (a group that helps women get help for postpartum depression and anxiety). These four women picked up the phone and called the 800 number. That is huge for me because those are four women who, hopefully, God willing, will get the help they need. Those are four mums who will enjoy their motherhood finally, and then those are four sets of children who will get their mum back. That to me is enormous, and such a privilege.

What is your favorite thing about your workspace?

I guess my kitchen is my workspace—the thing I love about it is that it's often full of people. Whether it's my daughter, or my husband, or my friends, when I'm cooking, it is a very social process. I love that. I love that I don't often have to work by myself. Physically, I love my spice wall in my kitchen. My husband made it for me, and it's a chalkboard and a spice wall in one. So I can write verses and words of encouragement on there for myself and then also grab my spices. I can see everything that I need.

Has learning from a mistake ever led you to success?

When I first won *Food Network Star*, I was coming at the whole thing from a place of such gratitude that it was almost a sense of *undeserved* gratitude. I think that shot me in the foot a little bit. I remember when my cooking show was canceled, I felt like, "But I did everything that you guys asked me to do." I remember being upset that the show had gone out in a way that I wouldn't have wanted it to. That helped me (after a long period of crying about it) to sort of reevaluate and realize I don't want to compromise who I am in order to be on TV. Something changes in you when you become a mum, where you're like, "No more BS. I don't

have time for this. I have a short period of time to be working, or else I'd like to go home." You become a freaking lioness about your children, but also about yourself and your time and your abilities because you want to be a good role model too. That has helped. I changed a lot about things I say yes to, things I say no to, and what I think is worth my time and what I think is not.

In moments of self-doubt or adversity, how do you build yourself back up?

Through my faith, really. My faith is a huge part of who I am and the things I'm able to do these days.

What quotation or saying inspires and motivates you to be yourself and do what you love?

There's a verse in Proverbs that says, "The righteous are as bold as a lion." And "righteous" just means "right living," and I know that I'm not always right living, but I'm inspired to live boldly because I only get one go at it.

What is your personal or professional motto?

"Eat, giggle, repeat" is on my website, but I'm starting to grow out of that a little bit. My big thing at the moment is, "Courage is not *not* feeling fear, but feeling fear and doing it anyway."

What would you tell yourself ten to twenty years ago that you wish you knew then?

I'm thirty-seven, so I would have been seventeen. . . . I would tell myself to do more. Like when I went to university—there are definitely classes I wish I had taken, like there was a whole class on freeing death row inmates and I never took it. And I so regret it now. But I also would tell myself to try really hard not to care so much about what other people think of you. It's not easy to do, and I think that's just part of growing up. I've talked to women in their fifties who say things like, "I don't give an F what anybody thinks about me anymore," and I think that's something that just comes with being fifty.

"Don't try to solve problems that don't yet exist."

Claire Mazur and Erica Cerulo

Entrepreneurs
New York, NY

What did you want to be when you were a child?

Claire: A multihyphenate: an ice skater–dancer–singer. And my parents were basically like, "Yeah, okay, cool. As long as you go to a four-year college, that's fine with us." And never once did they tell me it might be hard to do all three of those things, let alone be successful at one. So I really believed I could. And I think that concept—that I could be anything I wanted to be, no matter how outlandish—stuck with me and was a big part of why at twenty-six years old I was like, "Yes, I can totally launch my own business. Let's do this."

Claire Mazur (left) and Erica Cerulo

What was the best piece of business advice you were given when you were starting out?

Erica: When I told one of my risk-averse friends that Claire and I were going to take the leap and start this thing, she said that even if it crashed and burned, my résumé would be better off for it—that people respect those who have the nerve to strike out on their own and that it makes a good story.

What is your favorite thing about your workspace?

C: I love that the bones are white: the walls, the major furniture pieces, the fixtures. It means that all the pretty objects we bring into the space aren't competing for attention or crowding your visual field. We have so much stuff in here—products, samples, artwork—but it never feels cluttered or overwhelming.

Name a fear or professional challenge that keeps you up at night.

C: I spend a lot of time worrying about being a good manager. When you're in high school and you get elected student council president, it's like, "Great! I'm a natural-born leader. I've got this." Which: LOL. Being a leader is complicated and hard. And I tend to be pretty emotional and worry a lot about how I think other people might be feeling. Which, of course, makes me a better manager in certain situations, but I often wonder if I'd be more effective if I didn't spend so much time *caring*. I read an interview with Mindy Kaling where she said she was really inspired by female bosses who don't care what their staff thinks of them. And I remember thinking, God, that concept is so foreign to me.

Has learning from a mistake ever led you to success?

E: Launching an online business in 2010 in New York City, Claire and I felt a lot of pressure, I think, to operate like a start-up, not a small business—which meant going after investment and crazy-fast, hockey-stick growth. We tried to scale our business in ways that didn't totally make sense given our strengths, and we spent time, energy, and money chasing this dream we felt weird societal pressure to pursue. Once we let go of that, we felt more confident in the things we *are* really good at—and our ability to build on those things in really meaningful ways.

Name the biggest overall lesson you've learned in running a business.

E: Don't try to solve problems that don't yet exist. You could fill your head with so many "what ifs," but then there's no way you'd have the time, energy, or head space to deal with what's actually happening. For me, it's been hugely helpful to adopt a "we'll cross that bridge when we come to it" mind-set—not that I'm saying that it always (or ever?) comes easily.

What quotation or saying inspires and motivates you to be yourself and do what you love?

E: From the greatest motivator who ever was, Coach Taylor (*Friday Night Lights*): "You can't beat yourself up because you're taking chances on things."

Name your greatest success (or something you're most proud of) in your business experiences.

E: I'm super proud of the business partnership that Claire and I have built. We were friends for almost a decade before we started a company together, and growing our relationship in this direction has taken a lot of work—you know, kind of like a marriage. Five years in, I'm really impressed with what has evolved . . . and with what's stayed the same.

What does the world need more of?

E: More good vibes! We have a pretty strict don't-go-negative policy at Of a Kind. We aspire to be professional enthusiasts.

Name a woman (or women), past or present, whom you admire or look up to.

C: My mom. She's a scientist and a high-level executive. When I was growing up, I didn't fully grasp the nuances of what she did, but I had a sense that she was successful in a male-dominated industry and that the people who reported to her were mostly men. The number of times I wished she were a stay-at-home mom—and there were a lot of those, because most of my friends' moms didn't work—were far outnumbered by the times I felt really proud of her for being a badass.

> "Mix what you love to do with what you care about changing most."

Kathleen Hanna

Artist, Musician
New York, NY

What did you want to be when you were a child?
I took a career test when I was in seventh grade, and it gave me these numbers that corresponded to file folders with information about the top three jobs that would suit my personality. I'll never forget them: (1) dancer, (2) musician, (3) interior designer. Oddly, I ended up doing all three, being a musician and a dancer (stripping *does* count as dance, okay?) and going to Parsons for interior design, though I've only used my schooling for set design and random projects thus far.

What characteristic do you most admire in other creative women?
The ability to tell the difference between honest criticism and mean bullshit.

What does success mean to you?
Having people say my music turned them on to feminism or helped them deal with sexual abuse.

What is your favorite thing about your workspace?
That the door closes and locks and the beautiful mess behind it is all *mine*!!!

What is the biggest sacrifice you've made in your career/line of work?
Having to put up with overt and insidious sexist crap, keeping my voice in top shape all the time, and being away from the people I love when I tour.

Name a fear or professional challenge that keeps you up at night.
I don't like being treated like I'm a brand, but I have to navigate around the fact that some people think of me that way and try to turn it into a positive.

In moments of self-doubt or adversity, how do you build yourself back up?
I brag about my awesome accomplishments in my journal.

What quotation or saying inspires and motivates you to be yourself and do what you love?
"Being popular is overrated."

Which of your traits are you most proud of?
I can not only turn lemons into lemonade, I can turn lemons into Bundt cakes and sell them back to the people who used to terrorize me in high school.

What is your personal or professional motto?
Mix what you love to do with what you care about changing most.

What does the world need more of? Less of?
More food and shelter for people who live in poverty so they can participate in changing the world and making art. Less Wall Street criminals building ugly McMansions.

What would you tell yourself ten to twenty years ago that you wish you knew then?
To put my own oxygen mask on first before helping others.

> "I've got a playlist for any type of rut you can think of."

Sadie Barnette

Artist
New York, NY

What did you want to be when you were a child?

I think I wanted to be a writer; but I think in my head it was similar to being a detective. Definitely something with a briefcase. I probably imagined also wearing a crown of some type.

What was the best piece of business advice you were given when you were starting out?

One of my favorite artists and mentors, Andrea Bowers, told me no matter what, "just keep making art."

Name your greatest success (or something you're most proud of) in your business experiences.

Being an artist-in-residence at the Studio Museum in Harlem in 2015. The legacy, energy, and passion of this amazing program date back to 1968—to be a part of that history has been a great honor.

Name the biggest overall lesson you've learned in running a business.

It's all about the ideas. Even my ideas have ideas.

Has learning from a mistake ever led you to success?

In high school, I found I couldn't "succeed" at the confined expectations of the traditional school system. I stopped going to some of my classes and was on the path to fail to graduate. I switched to an independent study program and spent all my free time in a little darkroom there, where I discovered a passion for photography and, consequently, a reason to graduate and go on to college. Although it was stressful (and probably even more so for my mother), I simply could not conform to traditional high school and some part of me knew there had to be another way to be a person. Once I was at CalArts, I realized there was not something wrong with me, but something wrong with the system, and that there was a whole world of people with similar experiences who wanted to create new ways of learning and of recognizing excellence.

What is your no-fail go-to when you need inspiration or to get out of a creative rut?

Music! So much music . . . I've got a playlist for any type of rut you can think of.

Name a woman (or women), past or present, whom you admire or look up to.

Sarah Crowell and Kate Hobbs of Destiny Arts Center in Oakland, California.

> "It is important to be part of a community."

Anita Lo

Chef, Restaurateur
New York, NY

What did you want to be when you were a child?
When I was very young, I wanted to be a doctor like my mother. Then later I wanted to be a concert pianist (but lacked the drive and talent).

What was the best piece of business advice you were given when you were starting out? (Or a piece you're glad you ignored?)
David Waltuck told me not to open my own place. I still think that is very good advice and I tell my cooks in turn, as this is a hard business. I'm also glad I ignored it. You should get into this business only if your passions dictate that you must.

What is your favorite thing about your workspace?
The small size of my restaurant is ideal for ensuring the highest food quality.

What is the biggest sacrifice you've made in starting or running your business?
That's a hard question. A lot of blood, sweat, and tears go into opening a restaurant. You give up a social life for at least a year. You take on a lot of stress and responsibility. I worked for a few years with no pay and long hours, and then several more with very low pay. But the process is very exciting and was ultimately rewarding.

What does success mean to you?

Having a healthy, happy staff; happy, impressed customers; and a balanced life.

Name the biggest overall lesson you've learned in running a business.
Underpromise and overdeliver.

In moments of self-doubt or adversity, how do you build yourself back up?
I have a wonderful group of strong, female chef friends who are very supportive. It is important to be part of a community.

What quotation or saying inspires you and motivates you to be yourself and do what you love?
"Food brings people together."

Name your greatest success (or something you're most proud of) in your business experiences.
In 2009 my restaurant burned down and we had to close for nine months while we waited for the insurance to come through, for the renegotiation of our lease, and for the contractors to finish. In the end, even after that long period of time, all but one of my twenty-three or so employees came back to work (that one had taken a manager's position in the interim).

What does the world need more of? Less of?
More female fine-dining chefs with their own businesses. Less fear of foods from different cultures.

What's your favorite thing to come home to after a long day of work?
My partner, my two shih tzus, and my cat.

> "I'm most proud of my self-reliance. My basic message to myself has always been 'I can learn how to do this.'"

Ariele Alasko

Woodworker, Designer
Queens, NY

What did you want to be when you were a child?

When I was a kid I wanted to jump horses, and then for a while I wanted to be an Olympic speed skater, but I always knew I'd be an artist of some sort.

What was the best piece of business advice you were given when you were starting out?

"Don't be afraid to say no." I'm a huge fan of no. The best moves in my career came from quitting (saying no to) the things/jobs that were not really what I wanted, whether I had something else lined up or not. I think what this really means is, don't do anything you don't love or aren't totally excited by, and don't feel bad telling others that you're just not interested.

What is your favorite thing about your workspace?

It has to be the windows. I just recently moved and I've finally found a corner studio with windows on two sides—big drafty industrial windows with old chicken-wire glass panes. The light is beautiful, diffused, and bright all day.

Name the biggest overall lesson you've learned in running a business.

When I first started out on my own, I thought I had to follow the general rules, accepting orders and special commissions. I became a one-woman factory, and I was not enjoying it. I quickly realized that *not* following any business plan would be okay too, so I stopped fulfilling other people's wants and started making what I felt like making. In caring less about what people wanted, I noticed that people still cared about what I had to offer, and it also eliminated a lot of stress, as well as repetition and boredom.

Has learning from a mistake ever led you to success?

When I stumble across people copying specific pieces of my work or a friend's work almost exactly, I feel offended. So, my biggest lesson: I've stopped looking. It's no longer worth the distress and feeling all shaky over something that really doesn't matter. I don't look on Instagram anymore except for the few people I follow. Some days I'm honestly tempted to delete the app entirely and go back to the old days of paging through art books from the library. I've realized that it's easy to get stuck defending yourself; instead I've learned to pedal faster and not look behind myself.

What quotation or saying inspires and motivates you to be yourself and do what you love?

"Keep on truckin'."

Which of your traits are you most proud of?

I'm most proud of my self-reliance. My basic message to myself has always been "I can learn how to do this." I'm committed to learning everything for myself, although in many cases I fully acknowledge this to be extreme stubbornness. I still have no employees, by choice, because I prefer to do every step of the work on my own, even the grueling, repetitive, awful parts. But I'm proud of this! It makes me feel happy and independent.

The Women
at a Glance

Joy Cho
Designer and blogger at Oh Joy!
ohjoy.com
(page 272)

Anishka Clarke
Interior designer, co-owner of Ishka Designs
ishkadesigns.com
(page 321)

Danielle Colding
Interior designer, founder of Danielle Colding Design, Inc.
dcdny.com
(page 11)

Veronica Corzo-Duchardt
Graphic designer, founder of Winterbureau
winterbureau.com
(page 221)

Sibella Court
Interior designer, stylist
thesocietyinc.com.au
(page 188)

Amada Cruz
Chief curator and director of the Phoenix Art Museum
phxart.org
(page 136)

Cheryl Day
Co-owner of Back in the Day Bakery, coauthor of
The Back in the Day Bakery Cookbook
backinthedaybakery.com
(page 53)

Llubav Choy Duerr
Artist, illustrator
llubav.com
(page 266)

Carolina Ebeid
Poet, editor
carolinaebeid.com
(page 153)

Tina Roth Eisenberg
Designer; entrepreneur; founder of *swissmiss*,
CreativeMornings, and Tattly
swiss-miss.com
(page 284)

Carson Ellis
Artist, illustrator, author of *Home*, coauthor of
The Wildwood Chronicles
carsonellis.com
(page 307)

Cameron Esposito
Comedian, actor
cameronesposito.com
(page 119)

Carla Fernández
Designer, creative director and cofounder of
Carla Fernández
carlafernandez.com
(page 62)

Louise Fili
Graphic designer, founder of Louise Fili Ltd
louisefili.com
(page 171)

Eileen Fisher
Fashion designer, founder of Eileen Fisher, Inc.
eileenfisher.com
(page 254)

Lisa Folawiyo
Fashion designer, founder of Lisa Folawiyo
lisafolawiyo.com
(page 102)

Ashley C. Ford
Writer
ashleycford.net
(page 313)

Roxane Gay
Writer, professor, author of *Bad Feminist*
roxanegay.com
(page 85)

Hana Getachew
Textile designer, founder of Bolé Road Textiles
boleroadtextiles.com
(page 115)

Tavi Gevinson
Writer, founder and editor in chief of *Rookie* magazine
rookiemag.com
(page 20)

Kristina Gill
Development adviser, food editor/photographer
www.kristinagill.com
(page 296)

Nikki Giovanni
Poet, professor, acclaimed author of over thirty books
nikki-giovanni.com
(page 155)

Mary Going
Fashion designer, owner of Saint Harridan
saintharridan.com
(page 95)

Thelma Golden
Director and chief curator of the Studio
Museum in Harlem
studiomuseum.org
(page 39)

Photography
Credits

Principal photography by Sasha Israel, except for the following photographs:

Chloe Aftel: Page 343
Rinne Allen: Pages 52–53, 55, 86–87, 162–63, 165, 278–79, 280, 281, 331, 332, and 333
Jessica Bennett: Pages 245, 246, and 247
Christopher Bonney: Page 154
Annabel Braithwaite and Dorothée Brand: Pages 56 and 306
Roger Davies: Page 210
echo and earl: Pages 100, 106, 108, 109, 128–29, 130, 276, 334–35, and 336
Kirsten Ellis: Page 152
Kristina Gill: Page 297
Christian Harder: Pages 248 and 268–69
David Harrison: Page 197
India Hobson: Page 99
Ana Hop: Page 63
Sarah Hrudka: Pages 122–23, 125, and 157
Rick Levinson: Page 186
William Meppem: Page 189
The Oberports: Page 240
Lakin Ogunbanwo: Page 103
Aubrie Pick: Page 48
Anjali Pinto: Page 220
Robin Roemer: Pages 84 and 135
Anisa Rrapaj: Page 261
Michelle Smith: Pages 292–93
Alexandra Valenti: Pages 138–39
Lisa Warninger: Pages 136–37
Christina Wehbe: Pages 174–75
Matika Wilbur: Page 326
Michael Wilson: Pages 288–89
Claudia Zalla: Page 112

Acknowledgments

Not many people know that this book was *supposed* to be a massive DIY encyclopedia. The reason I was able to change plans, follow my dream, and turn it into a book about inspiring women is entirely because of Artisan's publisher, Lia Ronnen. Thank you, Lia, for believing in me as much as I believe in the women in this book.

The saying "It takes a village" has never been truer than with this project. A great deal of thanks is owed to women like Kari Stuart, Erin Abbott Kirkpatrick, Christy Pessagno, and Samantha Hahn, who went above and beyond to connect me with so many of these incredible women. Thank you to the entire Artisan family for their continued support: Shoshana Gutmajer, Sibylle Kazeroid, Allison McGeehon, Michelle Ishay-Cohen, Renata Di Biase, Nancy Murray, Mura Dominko, and everyone who helped bring this book to life.

Thank you also to Judy Linden and Christine Ragasa.

This book would not have happened without the help of Kelli Kehler. Her hard work, perseverance, patience, and love turned it from a very intimidating list of to-dos into a meaningful finished product. Thank you, Kelli.

Sasha Israel: There are *no* words to describe how thankful I am to have worked with you on this book. You made each shoot a joy and every one of us (in front of and behind the camera) feel comfortable and at home. You are a complete and total gift, and your photographs are more beautiful than I could have ever dreamed.

Thank you to Caitlin Kelch and the entire Design* Sponge team for all their support. I am so lucky to work with you all.

Thank you to my mom and dad for always supporting me. I love you both so much. Dad, thank you for being a part of such a special shoot.

Thank you to my mom- and dad-in-law, Doug and Rochelle Turshen. I am so lucky to have both of you in my life. Thank you for sharing your immense talents and guidance with this book.

Julia, Hope, Winky, and Turk: Thank you for every single day together. Our family and your love give me the motivation to keep working harder and dream bigger.

Last but not least, thank you to all the women who shared their stories for this book. Your words have inspired me endlessly, and I cannot wait for them to have the same effect on everyone who reads this. Thank you as well to your families—and your family pets (pictured at left)—for opening your homes and studios to us.

Grace Bonney is the founder of Design*Sponge, a daily website dedicated to the creative community. Design*Sponge was founded in 2004 and currently reaches over 1.5 million readers per day. A native of Virginia Beach, Bonney has worked as a contributing editor at publications such as *House & Garden*, *Domino*, and *Craft* magazine. She is passionate about supporting all members of the creative community; she runs an annual scholarship for up-and-coming designers, writes a free business column for creatives, and is the host of a weekly radio show, *After the Jump*. Her first book, *Design*Sponge at Home*, is a national bestseller. After twelve years in Brooklyn, Bonney now lives in New York's Hudson Valley with her wife and their three pets.